I Stand Corrected

ALSO BY EDEN COLLINSWORTH

It Might Have Been What He Said

I Stand Corrected

HOW TEACHING WESTERN MANNERS IN CHINA BECAME ITS OWN UNFORGETTABLE LESSON

Eden Collinsworth

NAN A. TALESE

Doubleday

New York London Toronto Sydney Auckland

www.nanatalese.com

DOUBLEDAY is a registered trademark of Random House LLC.
Nan A. Talese and the colophon are trademarks of Random House LLC.

Book design by Maria Carella
Jacket design by Gabriele Wilson
Jacket illustration by Roderick Mills/Heart Agency

Library of Congress Cataloging-in-Publication Data
Collinsworth, Eden.
I stand corrected : how teaching Western manners in China became its own
unforgettable lesson / Eden Collinsworth. —First edition.
pages   cm
ISBN 978-0-385-53869-5 (hardcover)
ISBN 978-0-385-53870-1 (eBook)
1. Collinsworth, Eden. 2. Business etiquette—Study and teaching—
China. 3. Businesspeople—Western countries—Social life and customs.
4. Etiquette—Western countries. 5. Etiquette—China. 6. Western
countries—Social life and customs. 7. China—Social life and customs.
I. Title.
HF5389.C653   2014
395.071'051—dc23   2014006096

MANUFACTURED IN THE UNITED STATES OF AMERICA

1   3   5   7   9   10   8   6   4   2

First Edition

TO MY FATHER, AND FOR MY SON

在家千般好，出门步步难.

You can be comfortable at home for a thousand days,
or step out the door and run into trouble.

—*Chinese proverb*

CONTENTS

I do not claim to be an expert on China, and though this book includes my personal opinions on that subject, it is an adventure story rather than an analysis. Everything I describe happened, but I have changed the names of some of the people. It was the polite thing to do.

I Stand Corrected

PROLOGUE

Wherein I prove it is sometimes possible to get away with folly

In the early 1980s, I was invited by a delegation of Chinese businessmen to visit Shenzhen. It was during China's progressive campaign of economic "opening up," and this former fishing village was growing into a booming metropolis constructed with what looked to be gigantic Lego pieces. At the time, I was twenty-nine. I was also tall, fair skinned, and redheaded, so when I arrived in Shenzhen, it was easy for the Chinese to believe I might have come not from America but from another planet entirely.

"What do you mean, he's asked how much I am?" was my stunned question to the colleague acting as my translator at a business dinner.

"Just that," he told me.

All at the table had been drinking a great deal of *baijiu*—distilled liquor with a high level of alcohol—and I asked my colleague if the man inquiring was sober.

"He seems to be," was the answer.

"Have you correctly translated?" I asked. "Surely he's asked how much it would cost to buy the company we represent."

"No. He means the cost for you, as a woman," reiterated my colleague. "Our guest has just inquired about taking permanent possession of you."

Latching on to whatever composure had not yet deserted me, I pointed out that I was not just a woman—I was also the president of a company. "One who happens to be the host this evening," I made clear.

"I can translate what you've just said," volunteered my colleague. "But it won't matter."

"Why not?" I wanted to know.

"Because he believes that your gender makes your professional rank insupportable."

And there it was. A full-in-the-face statement that forced upon me the irrefutable difference between my self-image and my status in China. Whatever I may have considered myself, I was at that time, in that place, a Western luxury item possibly to be purchased.

"What would you like me to tell him?" asked my colleague.

It took a moment before I realized it wasn't so much that I needed to surrender my self-image as that I should consider suspending it for the sake of what might be future business in China. Making a bottom-line calculation with that in mind, I responded with falsehoods calibrated to avoid embarrassment.

"First, thank him for his interest," I instructed my colleague. "Next tell him I am extremely flattered. And then let him know that, sadly, I belong to someone else."

Five years after a man in China tried to buy me, I gave myself away for free to another in my own country.

Marriage rewarded me with intoxicating happiness. It also pummeled me with impossibilities levied by a man I nonetheless adored. During a particularly desperate time—believing my husband would change course if he understood what was at stake—I spoke to him of separation. His response was starkly final. He left.

The end of our fifteen-year marriage unmoored my heart and stole my bearings. It also resulted in our eleven-year-old son, Gilliam, being left solely in my care. Inconsolable, I put my trust in time. And with time I realized that, despite the nonnegotiable requirement to support myself and Gilliam, I could choose what was next for us both.

It is often our subconscious self that underlies the choices we make. And so it must have been with my far-reaching decision to travel with Gilliam. That decision—more instinctive than cohesive—moved me off a single career path toward a wide vista of varied occupations. For the remaining years of Gilliam's adolescence, an e-mail service notified me each Wednesday of discounted airfares to international cities. By learning the system of last-minute hotel deals, I could afford to take us on a long weekend in a different foreign place every second month. Seamlessly changing countries, we became a nation of two.

Granted, it was an unorthodox way to raise a son, but there was a screwball comedy buoyancy about it. And nothing in our decade-long saga was as preposterous as the fact that it worked.

Given his upbringing, it wasn't entirely unexpected that at eighteen Gilliam, who was attending a Japanese school, chose to study Chinese at a British university. Two years later his academic program placed him at a Beijing university.

The Chinese have always revered education. Five hundred years before Christ, Confucius set in motion the ideal of rule by educated leaders, and the nature of China's educational system has been central to its cultural identity ever since. Making education available to the masses holds out the promise of upward mobility for anyone who can survive the rigors of study and examinations. But "survive" is the operative word. In China, college openings are limited, and students struggle under what translates to "the glory of high scores" in preparation for taking *gaokao,* the life-changing national college entrance exam. Gilliam observed that the extremely competitive nature of the Chinese system, the extraordinarily long hours of repetitive study, the expectation to conform and fit in, the lack of encouragement for creative expression—all of these factors seemed to create roadblocks for the young to achieve an advanced level of emotional intelligence.

He called me one day with an idea.

"I've come to the conclusion that China's school system is producing socially disconnected kids," he told me. "And I'm wondering if their parents would pay for an after-school program."

"What kind of program?" I asked.

"Classes for improvement in something like etiquette," he said.

We discussed Gilliam's business proposition until I remembered unpleasant news. My voice dropped when the subject changed.

"Bangkok is looking less likely for your birthday," I said in a sober tone.

"Something's happened," Gilliam guessed correctly.

"I'm afraid Sondhi's been shot," I told him.

"Is he dead?" asked Gilliam.

"Luckily, no. But his driver is."

"Mother, listen, I'm glad they haven't managed to kill Sondhi, but I'd like to live to see a few more of my birthdays, and the odds increase if I avoid your friends who incite riots in politically unstable countries."

It was a rather harsh reading of events, but I chose not to dispute my son's point. "All right, dear," was all I could think of saying. "If that's how you feel."

Several nights later I described the birthday dilemma at dinner with Jonathan, one of my less politically provocative friends.

"This man who invited you to Bangkok, what's his name?" Jonathan asked.

"Sondhi."

"Wasn't he the Thai media tycoon who financed your magazine in L.A.?"

"That's right. And now he's part of Thailand's yellow shirt movement," I explained.

"And there's someone else you knew targeted for assassination in another country."

"Neither was my fault, if that's where this is heading."

"Where was the other one—the one who was shot giving a speech?"

"East Timor."

"East Timor? Christ, Eden. How is it that you met these people on your own, before becoming involved with this . . . this . . . what is it?"

"A think tank," I answered. "A global think tank."

"Which does what exactly?" asked Jonathan.

"It handles conflict prevention," I told him.

"That's certainly working well," he quipped.

"Are you making fun of me?"

"No."

"Are you laughing at what I do?"

"This has nothing to do with what you do. This has to do with you thinking it's perfectly normal to celebrate your son's birthday with someone other people want dead."

"I didn't know that," I pointed out. And not wishing to dwell on a misrepresentation of my shortcomings, I shifted the conversation to the observations Gilliam had of his Chinese friends as socially ill equipped, and to how our phone conversation had led me to think on the larger issue of the East-West divide. I told Jonathan it seemed to me that, despite the growing status of China as a world economy and the unprecedented range of Chinese investments overseas, businessmen in mainland China—well educated and English speaking—were still uncomfortable in the company of their Western counterparts. I recalled my own ordeals of doing business among the Chinese and suggested that Gilliam's proposal for Western etiquette lessons in China was not without validity. I admitted to Jonathan that though my work as the chief of staff at a think tank was fascinating, it kept me on call in five international time zones, seven days a week. After four grueling years, I wasn't entirely opposed to recapturing my personal life and moving on.

"What would you say if I told you I was thinking of developing a program for Western business etiquette in China?" I asked.

Jonathan's expression spoke before words could. He put down his martini, uncrossed his legs, and shifted his weight to center himself for what had to be said. Locking his laser stare on me as if sanity itself were on trial, he asked a question posed by more people than I care to count during the course of my unruly life.

"Are you kidding?"

PART ONE

Introductions and Greetings

不笑莫开店.

A person without a smiling face must never open a shop.
—*Chinese proverb*

CHAPTER ONE

The word "etiquette" is rooted in the seventeenth-century gardens of Versailles—one of many reasons the French feel superior.

Set in a low valley between two lines of wooded hills, Versailles was the location for Louis XIII's hunting lodge, which he upgraded to château status. His son, Louis XIV—determined to build a lasting monument to his own regime—remolded the château to an over-the-top level of grandeur. That required a daily workforce of twenty-two thousand men and six thousand horses, and the exorbitant expense impoverished the country.

Before discontent among his citizens festered into rebellion, and rebellion triggered the Revolution, life at court was based on social rank. Versailles was entered by many different gates. Only the lucky few possessing the right to bring their coaches into the great courtyard of the Louvre were granted the right to enter Versailles by way of its main entrance. That left a large number of lower-tiered aristocrats with no immediate access.

When Louis XIV's gardener realized it was impossible to prevent those not invited through the front gate from trampling the lawns and flower beds, he put up signs. Already defensive about their lesser point of entry—fearing they were being left behind—the aristocrats ignored the postings, which resulted in a royal decree that no one go beyond the signs without a ticket, known in Old French as *etiquette.*

Louis XIV's insistence that his retinue uphold manners had an influence on the bourgeois, and the term *l'etiquette* became a broader reference to signs of correct behavior.

Temporarily banished during the French Revolution, etiquette was eventually recalled from exile and it still holds sway. When, after a joint press conference, French president Jacques Chirac muttered into—unbeknownst to him—an open microphone that British prime minister Tony Blair was *mal élevé,* those deadly two words formed the worst kind of insult. The expression translates to "badly brought up" and casts aspersions on not only the offender but also his parents.

Though not badly brought up, I certainly can't claim to be a trusted source on etiquette, but Gilliam's idea of Western etiquette lessons in China would not leave my imagination alone. It nagged at me until I decided to share the idea with a former colleague experienced in evaluating emerging markets. He, too, saw an opportunity.

My previous role as an executive at the Hearst Corporation included expanding its many brands. Prior to Hearst, I had implemented the same kind of brand-building strategy for *Buzz,* the L.A. magazine I launched. With contributing editors ranging from Jan Morris to Edmund White, *Buzz* built a reputation for its editorial quality. My partners and I were quick to leverage that reputation by launching *Buzz Weekly,* an arts and entertainment guide, by establishing Buzz On-Line, and by founding Buzz Books.

In order to pursue Gilliam's idea in China, we would first need to build a platform of brand recognition there. *What about a book on Western business comportment for the Chinese?* I thought. Not too unlikely a consideration, but one requiring a next step.

A train of incidents moved me forward: I'd written a novel published the year before. . . . My literary agent, based in London, had an associate in Beijing. . . . That associate was taken by the idea of a book for Chinese about Western business comportment.

In a combined state of ignorance and enthusiasm, I resigned as chief of staff at the think tank and moved to Beijing during Gilliam's summer break.

That way madness lies, as the English would say, and I would have to agree—it was a fairly mad thing to do. Without a guaranteed source of income, I would be living off my savings; I didn't speak Chinese; and I am far from an authority on manners. In point of fact, this is where I admit to several nasty tendencies, including a knee-jerk reaction to verbally wound those I think deserve the worst of me after they have tortured the best of me, which is my patience. That said, I've always made an effort to veer away from bad behavior and move toward the common sense that is good comportment. I do so because it is a shrewd approach to business and because I believe that there is value in the social contract humans have with one another.

To a large degree, our beliefs are instilled by our parents. My parents were of the mind that upholding values required honorable action but, when all else failed, it was sensible to leave the premises. Both were only children who never returned to their places of origin.

My father left the South to attend Harvard Business School. His only relative in the North was Sherman Billingsley. After a stint in Leavenworth during Prohibition for distributing liquor in the drugstores he bought for that purpose, Billingsley redeemed himself by creating the Stork Club, a glamorous gathering place for café society in New York.

My mother was old-world European and a different kind of exile. Like her own mother, she was mentally ill. She was also impeccably mannered. I managed to hold these distinct and, at times, contradictory ideas in my head while sepia-toned propriety dispelled the larger disquiet of what became her progressively frequent stays in mental institutions. She would disappear and then reappear, as if nothing were out of place but time. The fact that she committed herself was never discussed or, indeed, acknowledged.

If my professional career carries a credit balance, it can be found in my childhood. The intense ecosystem that was my family consisted of my parents, my two brothers, and me. But there was another, hidden member of our family: silence. And odd as it sounds, our implicit agreement to ignore that which was so obviously wrong enabled me, when it came time, to understand the Asian principle of saving face. It was also my childhood—with its forced introduction to the complexities of human nature—that would equip me, as an adult, to work with a disparate range of people, some considered completely impossible by most others.

My father was a success in business. He was also an ethically exacting man. Believing that financial dependency wove a sticky web of complacency, he put my inherited privilege on a timer. Until twenty-one, I was safeguarded by advantages but expected to behave within the strict confines of a nonnegotiable correctness—one that forced my mother's mental illness to hide beneath the surface. Given my remove from the wider world, the only opportunity to learn about the metaphorical scheme of things came from observing anything within my limited line of vision.

Improbable as it may seem, that included Maria Callas.

My father's board meetings provided family forays from our home in Chicago to a hotel in New York where his company's suite was directly across the hall from the one Aristotle Onassis kept for Callas during the better part of his marriage to Jackie Kennedy. Callas was my equivalent of what Flaubert must have encountered on his first trip to Egypt. Her physical being—splashed in bold, Picasso-like strokes—was wonderfully different from anything I had known. Having been confined to a life of nuance, I was fascinated by the theatrical exaggeration of hers. Never-ending activity swirled around her. A personal maid coordinated every form of room service. Floral deliveries arrived almost on the hour, and several times a day her white toy poodle—whose coat was trimmed like topiary—was handed to one of the bodyguards for its walk.

There was a menacing kind of glamour to Onassis's arrival, announced by the guttural sounds of armed security men who—my mother was quick to point out—didn't know enough to remove their hats while in the elevator.

"An ugly little man," was her appraisal of Onassis. "Contemptuously unapologetic for the inconvenience he causes the other guests."

My mother's observation was not incorrect. Onassis was a physically unattractive man. Far more interesting to me at thirteen was another fact, just as obvious: Onassis was a married man. That made Callas his mistress. At a time when that word had consequences, one might have thought the degree to which it was public would force a corresponding sense of embarrassment on her. That's what should have happened according to the code of conduct by which I was brought up. But Maria Callas did not appear chastened. Quite the opposite. She was having an extremely good time, and that third irrefutable fact permitted me to consider that life need not be coded to what others believed to be proper behavior.

Just as it was with my brothers, the vacuum sound of my father's bank vault closing was heard as I was handed a college diploma. Having no choice in either matter, I had been raised to be—in equal parts—ladylike and employable. The former prepared me for who knows what; the latter provided a lifeline to self-reliance.

At twenty-one, my ambitions were focused on New York, but dismal typing skills undermined my opportunities there. I took the only job available to me at the time: a substitute receptionist answering phones at the book publishing company Doubleday.

Most callers don't automatically announce themselves, so time after time I was forced to say, "May I ask who is calling?" The second day on the job, that straightforward question might have been reason enough for me to be told not to return for a third day.

"Whoever you are, hang up the phone so I can call back and leave a message," were the gruff instructions from an unannounced caller.

"I think you'll find me capable of taking a message," I suggested glibly. "The first thing I would ask is the name of the person calling. Who may I ask is calling now?"

The ominous silence that followed led me to believe I might have overstepped myself.

The literary agent Candida Donadio was a maverick with no formal education but unerring instincts for identifying talent. She was born on October 22, 1929, a date, it is said, memorialized in *Catch-22* and explained by the fact that Joseph Heller was her client. He was but one of them: Thomas Pynchon, William Gaddis, Philip Roth, John Cheever, Peter Matthiessen, Nelson Algren, and Christopher Isherwood—all were, in some part, due to Candida.

A botched phone ploy brought us together.

Trying to avoid talking to the Doubleday editor to whom she owed a call, Candida had hoped that, by leaving a message on the machine, she would be relieved of any further obligation. Instead, she got me.

Candida was known to like a drink, and the several that had preceded her call allowed the barriers to slip long enough for her to suggest not that she have me fired but that we should meet. The suggestion was out of character for her: Candida was a semirecluse. "To trust is good," she would tell me, and then she would add, "Not to trust is better." Ignoring the width of our age gap, we became close friends. It was she who persuaded me to stake a career in book publishing.

Impossible to have imagined, but eight years after my first job as a receptionist—by way of a great deal of luck and relentlessly hard work—I became the head of another publishing company, Arbor House, which, at the time, was part of the Hearst Corporation. Despite my off-topic introduction to Chinese business practices in Shenzhen shortly after I was named publisher, China intrigued me enough to return a year later—by myself and without the intent of doing business.

Lured by its 1920s glamour, I spent a week in Shanghai's old Cathay Hotel, whose rooms—festooned with gold silk and lacquered in red—were suffused with an aura of the past. Each afternoon, I took tea in the lobby among the ghosts of courtesans and gangsters. And when it came time to return to New York, I was determined that—be it on business or for the sake of travel—I would come back.

I did.

Revisiting Shanghai several years later, I took a bullet train from the airport to the center of the city. What fueled my disbelief was not that I was being hurtled ahead at two hundred and sixty-eight miles an hour on the thin layer of air between the train and the magnetized narrow tracks; far more disconcerting was what I saw when we slowed down and I looked out the window: some of the peasants—knee-deep in rice paddies—were on cell phones.

Entering the telecommunications market with satellite-based platforms, China managed to leapfrog over the first generation of cable-based systems in the West, and now over 75 percent of its 1.3 billion–plus people have at least one cell phone.

It could be the sheer number of people in China trying to have their say, but shrill voices—often combined with spittle spray—come across several decimals higher than is comfortable to Westerners. Noise accompanies one everywhere in China; there is practicality to the customary phone greeting *wei,* which means "Can you hear me?" or "Is anyone there?"

Even after my third trip to China, the country continued to baffle. Its social rules were puzzling. Its business agreements were revocable. Its people were accessible and, at the same time, unreachable. Whenever a Sinophile would explain Chinese culture, my response was always the same polite "I see," although I didn't quite. Chinese history was too full of incident for a tidy explanation. I wanted a better understanding, and my mind kept circling back.

Like a complicated mathematical equation I was determined to solve, China called me back numerous times over the next twenty-five years. There came many adventures, but only one revelation: I would remain forever and beguilingly mystified by the Middle Kingdom.

CHAPTER TWO

China—or Zhongguo, the Middle Kingdom—was designated in name during the Zhou dynasty in 1000 B.C. The early
Chinese believed that they were living in the middle ground of
the earth, surrounded by barbarians.

When China's flag was hoisted above Tiananmen Square
in the fall of 1949, the Communist Party extended the country's official name to its full reach: Zhonghua Renmin Gong-
heguo, or the Middle Glorious People's Republican Country.
Plain English stripped away the self-promotional embellish-
ment, reducing the nation's identity to the People's Republic
of China.

I first set my sights on China in the 1980s, some fifteen
years after the Cultural Revolution had unleashed a decade
of chaos. By then the Communist Party had abandoned Mao
Zedong's ideological zealotry and was marching in lockstep
behind the ever-pragmatic Deng Xiaoping, who thought
China's future rested on its ability to build a middle class and
whose campaign of radical transformation set the stage for the
nation's frenzied transition to state-sanctioned capitalism.

The 1990s in China featured political leaders who proved
remarkably skillful at appearing to adhere to the Maoist notion
of learning from the people but who had no intention of giving them a collective voice. I watched as the one-party system
managed political catastrophes that threatened to loosen the

Communists' tight grip on the levers of power, including a violent demonstration in Tiananmen Square that shook the pillars of the party's legitimacy.

Twenty-four years later, President Xi Jinping declared his admiration for Mao's legacy by banning seven "subversive" topics of discussion in universities, including Western ideas of democracy, alternative judicial systems to those in China, the promotion of universal values of human rights, Western-inspired notions of media, civic participation, and ardently promarket neoliberalism.

Some foreign observers speculate that Xi—the son of a revolutionary veteran—has made a strategic decision to preserve the nationalist base within the Communist Party and that, by consolidating his power, he has provided enough cover to implement China's much-needed market reforms. That would be good for us all, since the future of the world is the future of a global economy, and no other nation will succeed fully if China is held back. More than ever before, economic outcomes are the result not just of markets but of global politics and policy.

China—the world's largest nation—is facing its own policy-related conundrum. In order for China to underwrite its political and social order, the Communist Party must continue to deliver growth. For growth to continue, two things must occur: the Chinese judicial system must find a way to guarantee the protection of private assets, and sooner rather than later, the Chinese financial system must accept further liberation.

In 2013, President Xi signaled the party's willingness to gradually wean its economy off state subsidies and to allow the market a greater hand in setting prices. But economic reform is a multifaceted process, and China's internal challenges cannot be successfully addressed by preventing open dialogue at institutions of higher learning.

The seventh forbidden topic of debate in universities is criticism of the party's traumatic past—a more grievously short-sighted ban than the other six, it seems to me. By denying its past mistakes, China remains a poor student of its own lessons. I don't claim the expertise to conjecture the future of China, but there is something to the idea that in order to move forward, it is often necessary to first look back.

I have to believe that, at some point, the Chinese will find the wisdom to acknowledge the deep self-inflicted wounds of the Great Leap Forward and the Cultural Revolution. Those human catastrophes gouged down to the bone of China's identity, severing intellectual lifelines and denying the Confucian orthodoxy of family over state that had formed China's cultural foundation for more than a millennium.

Confucian principles stress the importance of hierarchical relationships in achieving a stable and harmonious society. These relationships are centered on deference to a dominant figure in a system of behaviors and ethical obligations that cascade down in order of priority: ruler and subject; husband and wife; parent and child; brother and sister; friend and friend. Each of these relationships requires an appropriate show of deference.

Born in 551 B.C., Confucius was largely unknown during his lifetime. After his death, those of his disciples who had mastered his teachings compiled his reflections and sayings in the *Analects*. During the centuries that followed, Confucianism was both revered and vilified, depending on the political backdrop , but it found enough footing to form the philosophical foundation on which the reverence of education and leadership coexisted in China.

"Aspire to the principle, behave with virtue, abide by benevolence, and immerse yourself in the arts"—these are the four tenets at the core of Confucius's teachings. Whether any of them has a place in contemporary China—or, for that matter, the modern world—is difficult to know, but it cannot be disputed that Confucianism has had a long and penetrating influence in China. *The Rites of Zhou*, one of Confucianism's three classic texts on ritual, names forbearance as the root of harmony and identifies deference as the cause of prosperity. Dating from the mid-second century B.C.—and enjoining the importance of family, a reverence for age, and kindness to strangers—it outlines moral principles that form the basis of Chinese law.

Mao—obsessed with ridding China of what he named its bourgeois elements—force-marched the Chinese away from their cultural touchstones and ancestral bonds. The Cultural Revolution replaced the Confucian virtue of deference with the authority of the Red Guards, made up first of students, some still in elementary school, and then of workers; last to join the ranks were soldiers. Purged were the Four Olds: old customs, culture, habits, and ideas. Professors, teachers, students, writers, and scientists were targeted for reeducation, given no choice but to prove their allegiance through self-condemnation. One survivor described it as "the physical and mental liquidation of oneself." Those identified as enemies of the regime faced firing squads. Those not killed—or who did not commit suicide—were dispersed to work on farms or in labor camps. Those unable to resist the pressure denounced their neighbors as enemies of the cause. No one dared trust anyone other than family—a mentality still apparent, particularly in the ways Chinese conduct their business affairs.

Some of my colleagues in China were children at the time of the Cultural Revolution. How they survived its physical brutality and emotional deprivation I shall never know. Nor can I imagine the sacrifices of which they rarely speak—sacrifices rarely spoken of because enmeshed in the Chinese culture is an overriding sense of collective responsibility that prevents individual self-expression.

It took nine years after meeting me for a friend to admit she had seen her father beaten to death. And a decade passed between us before a colleague, the CFO of a state-owned TV station, stoically described the afternoon he was robbed of his childhood. With words devoid of self-pity but in a voice that conveyed the ever-renewable sting of abandonment, he told me that, at the age of ten, he returned home from school one day to learn that his parents had been taken away to be reeducated. He was assigned the duty of smashing the heads off Buddha statues before he was assigned factory work in another province.

Destroying any book, artifact, or scripture associated with China's cultural past, the Cultural Revolution bled out the country's history. Tombs were vandalized and temples were demolished. Much of China's ancient heritage disappeared, along with the Chinese practices of etiquette. Unlike the French, who temporarily denounced the supremacy of manners during a violent but relatively short burst of revolution, the Chinese expunged theirs under Mao's claim of progress.

DONGZHIMEN IS THE location of what once was Beijing's northeast city gate that led to the countryside. As proof of the city's rapid transformation, the vicinity is now central Beijing. Housing there ranges from Soviet-style walk-ups to high-end luxury villas. In the morning, newly minted office workers wait for city buses, while impatient rich in their posh cars honk at migrant peasants in horse-drawn carts. By the late afternoon, trees are swollen with the hypnotic buzzing of cicadas, and sidewalks become littered with tradespeople napping on collapsed cardboard boxes. At night, those same sidewalks are lit by the slow glow of flame burners from the food stalls. Noodle soup bubbles in large vats, skewers of meat and chicken sizzle on grills, flaky pastries make an appearance, and Dongzhimen—seen under its hanging red lanterns—becomes a trove of dining possibilities.

Determined to experience adventure at the ground level, Gilliam and I were foreigners, or *laowai,* among the locals in Dongzhimen the summer I decided to settle in Beijing. We moved into a middle-class Chinese compound, where our semi-Westernized apartment featured two small bedrooms, an equally small kitchen with a washing machine, an enclosed porch with a pulley system to hang clothes to dry, and two bathrooms with sitting toilets rather than the customary squatting facilities. Neighbors on our floor were three young Chinese couples, each with a single child and at least one set of live-in grandparents.

In my previous travels, translators had shielded me from the fact that very little English is spoken in Beijing outside its universities and office buildings. With several years of Mandarin behind him, Gilliam was fairly fluent. I was proud of his achievement, but my dependency on it created an uncomfortable role reversal—beginning with our mandatory visit to the police station in Dongzhimen.

The Maoist-era residency permit known as *hukou*—with which people are identified according to their place of birth—continues to function in China as a way to control migration from rural to urban areas. Residents over sixteen are issued a *hukou* by the Ministry of Public Security; any foreigner not staying in a hotel but living in China beyond a specified duration must provide proof of residency.

Police departments in China operate under the jurisdiction of the Ministry of Public Security. The relationship between the police and the people is a close one; police stations are community centers of sorts, where neighborhood information is disseminated and minor disputes are settled. Armed with our passports and the apartment lease, Gilliam and I arrived at our local station prepared to do the right thing under Chinese law.

As the head of household, I was handed the all-important form, which was in Chinese and featured boxes to be checked. Gilliam read the choices out loud.

"There's no box for a three-month stay," I said once I'd heard all of the choices.

"Check the one for one year," instructed Gilliam.

"No," I told him. "We'll put an asterisk by the one-year box with a footnote on the bottom of the page indicating that ours is a three-month stay."

"There's no such thing as an asterisk or a footnote in Chinese," my son pointed out.

"Well, improvise," I said.

"You don't improvise here," he told me.

"Why not?" I asked.

"It's not in the Chinese mentality," said Gilliam.

"I don't care about the Chinese mentality. I'm not signing a legal document that contains a falsehood," I made clear.

Gilliam's patience began its retreat.

"You'll cause more trouble by deviating from the form," he said sharply. "The desk person will report us to his supervisor, and we'll be here for hours."

"But I'll be doing something illegal if I check the one-year box," I insisted.

"Mother, trust me on this. Everything is slightly illegal in China. That's the point."

Not until I'd lived in China for a while did I understand that—by the letter of the law—everything *is* slightly illegal in China. And yes, that is precisely the point: when called on to suppress political dissent, the authorities can cite any number of recorded infractions—including misrepresenting oneself on a registration form, as I did. I did something slightly illegal at the state-run police station in order to submit their stamped form at the state-owned bank . . . in order to receive a state-issued card, which would enable me to turn on the state-managed electricity in our apartment . . . so that we were not left in the dark.

Despite my willingness, there were times during my first few weeks of living in Beijing that I didn't fully comprehend what was happening, even after it happened. Still, I did my best when it came to *ru xiang sui su,* a practice of following the local customs.

Some of the customs were too subtle to notice. The obvious ones seemed driven by unbridled superstition. A single-digit number disappeared an entire floor in our apartment building. Dangerous to have a fourth floor, I was told. In Chinese, the word for the number 4 sounds too similar to the word for death. So seriously is the homophonous relation taken that the number rarely appears in financial projections for fear of bad luck in business. On the other hand, the number 8, which is pronounced much the same as the word for prosperity, is highly coveted, and people pay to ensure its appearance in their phone numbers and on their license plates. Hotel rooms with the number 8 are especially popular with business travelers.

With or without the advantage of lucky numbers, one should not invite adventure into one's life without being willing to tolerate some degree of uncertainty. Chinese superstition was not my only challenge. Several days after arriving, I felt a single, painful lump under my arm. I assumed it was a large spider bite until, the next day, a second lump in the same location appeared under my other arm. Gilliam acted as translator while the local pharmacist explained that the underarm lumps were my lymph nodes, knotted defensively by my immune system, which was under attack from Beijing's pollution—pollution so bad that not only could I taste particles of iron from the city's nonstop construction, but when the winds picked up, my eyes were stung by a fine powder of topsoil from Beijing's defoliated outskirts.

Each morning, I woke to a solid mass of humidity and a sun, devoid of color, that curded the sky's milky clouds. Beijing's haze stagnated at a headache-inducing level, while the city groaned under the weight of its expansion. Weeks of thick pollution and stifling heat produced various forms of discomfort. There were divides between what I could live with and what I could not but was forced to.

Cupping is an ancient form of alternative medicine believed to mobilize blood flow and heal a wide variety of ailments. In the hot weather, my queasiness at the more publicly lurid signs of cupping—inky-purple spherical bruises and red welts on bare backs—contributed to the impression that I was living in a radically weird place.

Out of my element, I found certainty in keeping a neat and orderly house—my way of feeling more comfortable when the sheer foreignness of my surroundings has pushed me beyond my limits. I learned to cook unidentifiable vegetables recommended by farmers who had traveled for hours to sell their produce from the makeshift stalls in the neighborhood. I hired what is called an auntie to help with the cleaning, washing, and ironing. Gilliam was assigned the responsibilities of maintaining our supply of drinking water and making sure our computer continued to function. Without a television or radio, the apartment's erratic Internet connection provided our limited but only access to the outside world. The years at a global think tank had trained my eye on the world's current events, but when I learned that the sites of *The New York Times,* CNN, the BBC, and Google were periodically blocked, it was surprisingly easy for me to adjust to a life of less information.

While everything in China is slightly illegal, the corollary is also true: anything in China is possible. A visible sign of this is the adjustable rules by which people obtain permission to buy and drive cars in Beijing.

To reduce the pea-soup pollution that envelopes the city, the Beijing government has restricted the use of passenger cars in the main area of the city. The final of seven digits on a license plate determines the days the car may not be driven. The rich beat the system by buying second cars and registering them under their drivers' names.

In the 1980s, when I first came to China, only government officials were allowed to have cars. Now Beijing has implemented a lottery system to control the number of new cars on the road. Unsurprisingly, the rich are able to sidestep the lottery with bribes, while others wishing to own a car must add their names to a pool of one million hopefuls. Each month, ten thousand lucky numbers are drawn for permission to obtain license plates—but a drastically smaller number of those new car owners in Beijing actually know how to drive.

Traffic lights, no matter what color, are largely ignored. Lane markers serve no real purpose. It is not uncommon for drivers who've missed their exits to simply put their cars in reverse and back up into oncoming traffic. U-turns are made in the middle of streets. At times, passing is done by way of the sidewalk. The mentality among drivers is simple: if you see me, you are responsible for not hitting me; if I don't see you, it's not my fault if I hit you. Occasionally, traffic police are stationed on elevated platforms at overconverged junctions. In the middle of the chaos, they appear oddly removed from their purpose, like prairie dogs stiffly standing at alert, surveying the traffic and doing nothing about it.

One can measure Beijing's dribble-down economy by how difficult it has become to get a cab when there are so many of them on the street. Government-subsidized gas results in incredibly cheap fares, which, in turn, result in the promiscuous use of cabs by China's ever-increasing middle class. Cabdrivers find better-paying jobs in a matter of weeks, and openings behind the wheel are filled by peasants from the country unsure of their way around Beijing, a city whose façade and boundaries are in a constant state of alteration.

My preferred means of transport was the onomatopoeic tuk-tuk: a two-wheeled, open-sided rickshaw attached to the back of an electric bicycle. But even tuk-tuks get snarled in Beijing's unbelievable traffic jams. We were fortunate to be living in a neighborhood where we could walk to wherever we needed to go.

During the day, sidewalks surrounding our compound were flecked with collapsible kiosks, each under the stewardship of a man offering a single service: some repaired sorry-looking bicycles; others patched tuk-tuk tires; others resoled shoes; still others struggled to give renewed life to what appeared to be mechanical appliances left behind from the 1940s.

By six o'clock, the aromas of roasted meat, ginger, garlic, and spices hung almost visibly in the air. Replacing the fruit and vegetable stands were tiny family-owned restaurants. With no more than two or three tables, diners slurped their meals shoulder to shoulder. Each restaurant featured its own specialty dish so inexpensive that it was cheaper to eat out every night than to buy the ingredients to cook. *"Fuwuyuan!"* Gilliam would call out to get anyone's attention. "Service worker!" is the to-the-point translation; there are no Chinese words for "Excuse me, may I have . . ."

Going about my uncomplicated life in Beijing, I was surrounded with a sometimes overwhelming collection of humanity. And though the Chinese have never appeared to me to be people who easily lose hope, I saw too many failures in the system to accept China's baseline approach to governing: that ideological thinking is what matters. Nor could I help wondering how one holds on to one's soul in a place where political beliefs designate human labor a commodity.

The day I tripped over a corpse on the sidewalk was the day of my deepest despair. The hundred yuan—the equivalent of about sixteen dollars—I gave the young man who was begging for money to bury his mother didn't keep me from weeping once I got home. But China is not where the welfare of one is the welfare of all; neither is it a place for Westerners to voice their political convictions. And so I focused my determination on what I went there to do.

One month after arriving in Beijing, I'd completed an outline and sample chapters for a book whose translated title was *The Tao of Improving Your Likability: A Personal Guide to Effective Business Etiquette in Today's Global World.* The Chinese concept of Tao (also referred to as Dao) signifies a designated route. My own Tao was not yet clear. Manuscript in hand, I flagged a tuk-tuk for the bumpy ride to my Chinese agent's office—and to whatever was next.

CHAPTER THREE

My agent scheduled meetings with four different editors interested in publishing my book.

Each greeting required one of us to do something unnatural to the other. While shaking hands is a welcomed requirement among Westerners, it is an uncomfortable practice for the Chinese. When meeting Westerners for the first time, the Chinese almost always avoid eye contact. And though a smile comes easily for a Westerner, the Chinese consider smiling at someone you don't yet know too familiar and therefore impolite.

From a Chinese perspective, Western men—with their overly enthusiastic display of good cheer—are inappropriately familiar when they place their hands on shoulders or backs in a gesture of bonhomie. On the occasions that Europeans lunge forward to kiss both checks, Chinese women become frozen in panic.

Most Chinese offer little more than reserve during their greetings: no smiles, no eye contact, and a minimum of touching. You would be right to think this does not radiate warmth. But introductions are put in perspective by cultural surroundings. Making the effort to observe, one can take a cue from what appears in plain sight—for greetings, no matter where they take place, are foreshadowed by body language.

It has been my observation that North Americans and

Europeans are comfortable standing two or, at the most, three feet apart from the person they are greeting or speaking to, but that South Americans and Indians are likely to get closer, while the Chinese—who are loath to make eye contact—seem to have found a way of eliminating personal space entirely. It has also come to my attention that the English generally do not display a great deal of physical contact with strangers, friends, or—from what I have seen—their spouses or children. France seems to me a country where people shake hands most often and in all situations—women and children included—as it is considered a sign of equality. I have learned, however, not to presume that the French are particularly interested in speaking to anyone who is not French. Not many geographical miles away, the Italians instinctively offer kindness over recrimination. In Italy, spoken words are their own melodic reassurance, hand gestures range freely into associations, and you venture to fill in the blanks.

As for the handshake, it is said to date back to Babylonian times, when men—proved to be the more aggressively ill-mannered gender—extended the open right hand to show that they were not holding a weapon, which might explain why the gesture was not required between a man and woman until relatively modern times. It is my belief that the genesis of the handshake remains as germane now as it was then, for modern man has given modern woman any number of excellent reasons for her to be approaching him with a sharp object in hand.

A veritable bar code of information for a Westerner, the way one shakes another's hand conveys a great deal of information quickly. When Gilliam was a boy of six, I taught him how. We were living in L.A. at the time.

A lesson for a youngster is far more effective when camouflaged as a game. Games feature the same set of components presented in the same sequence. First, there is a presentation of possibilities, dictated by the rules of the game. Next there is a single choice of action made by the player. Finally, there is the revelation of a correct or incorrect choice. Congratulations come with the former; encouragement to repeat the game offsets the disappointment of the latter.

Like any other game, my handshake game started with an underlying premise: women are different from men and require a different handshake.

"Does that mean you have one handshake and I'll have two?" asked Gilliam, alert to a possible inequity in the division of labor.

"That's right," I said. "I shake a man's hand exactly as I'd shake a woman's because I'm a woman. Not only that, because I am a woman, it is up to me to decide if I want to shake a man's hand."

"A girl made this up," Gilliam said, crossing his arms.

"Why would you think that?" I asked, trying not to sound defensive.

"Because girls are bossy and they like to make the rules."

His playground observation was fundamentally correct.

"You're probably right," I conceded. "But because you're the boy, you will have more chances at decoding the messages in the handshakes."

"What kind of messages?"

"Well, each handshake has a message that tells you something about the person. The more you shake hands, the better you get at decoding. But first we have to code your own handshake."

Curiosity took hold. "How do we do that?" asked Gilliam.

"You need to decide what you want to say about yourself," I told him. "Your handshake is a way of saying it without words."

"Do you mean what I want to be when I grow up?"

"Okay, that's one way of thinking about yourself. So what do you want to be?" I asked.

Our recent bedtime reading had been Greek mythology. Without hesitating, Gilliam answered, "A god."

"I think what you are saying about yourself is that you want to be considered important. Someone to pay attention to. So you should shake a man's hand with confidence. One tug down"—I took his small hand in mine—"like this. Not up-and-down and up-and-down, but just once—a little up and more down and then let go. It will be a signal that you mean business. And be sure to look him in the eye."

We practiced a few times before I thought Gilliam was ready for the ladies' handshake.

"Remember, women are different," I said. "You take their hand if they extend it, and then you shake gently."

In his eagerness to get on with it, Gilliam suggested we practice both versions.

"Before we do, would you like me to tell you a riddle?"

Willingness stretched only as far as the issue at hand. "Does it matter?" he asked impatiently.

"I think it does. But maybe you're too young to be told. Maybe we should wait."

"Tell me," he insisted.

I lowered my voice. "All women like one thing. This one thing is so precious that it doesn't have a price."

Gilliam's brow knotted in concentration.

"No amount of money can buy it," I continued. "But—here's the riddle—it's also free."

"What? What's free that every woman wants?" he wanted to know.

"Women want men to treat them like ladies."

"How do you do that?" he asked, ready to do what it took.

"Like everything, it starts with the handshake," I said, inviting him back into the game. "When you shake a woman's hand, make the slightest bow. Remember King Arthur's tales? His knights bowed to the ladies. Not too much of a bow . . . a half bow. A little chivalry goes a long way. I'll tell you what, you stand behind the door, and when you knock, I'll open it, but you won't know whether I'm pretending to be a man or a woman until I say."

He knocked on the door. I'd open it, saying either "I'm a man, how do you do?" in an artificially deep voice or "I'm a woman, how do you do?" The game lasted until Gilliam felt confident.

For months afterward, he sailed effortlessly from one gender-specific handshake to the next, until his father—who had written a play—brought him along to pick up the manuscript pages from his typist, whose name was Phyllis. What had not been clear until his second encounter with Phyllis was that she was not completely a she. Phyllis—previously Phil—was in between, so to speak. She was what is known as an "early tranny," a transsexual who had added breasts but had not yet subtracted the last—and most vital component—of manhood.

Phyllis opened the front door to her East Hollywood bungalow, took one look at Gilliam, and, in words textured by crushed velvet intonations, asked, "How do *you* do?"

Greeted by a person whose appearance didn't seem to rest securely in one gender, the boy quickly abandoned any attempt at a cognitive decision on which handshake to employ. Acting on instinct, he hid behind his father. That night, after considering the issue from both sides, Gilliam volunteered that, if there were to be another occasion to greet Phyllis, he would give her a slight bow, because—regardless of what gender she was—one thing was obvious: Phyllis wanted to be treated like a lady.

PART TWO

The All-Important Display of Deference

不患无位, 患所以立.

Do not worry about holding a high position, worry rather
about playing your proper role.

—*Confucius*

CHAPTER FOUR

Arithmetic is on the side of China.

The huge nation—with 20 percent of the world's population—has an unprecedented range of overseas investments projected to be worth between $2 trillion and $3 trillion by 2020, a state-sanctioned bank that supplies over half the world's total liquidity, and a self-appointed government that seeks access to global markets and resources.

Chipping away at not only the edifice of America's global dominance but also its self-belief, China's state-owned firms have sought out iconic Western companies for direct investment, taking stakes in Greece's largest port, Portugal's biggest power plant, London's Heathrow Airport, the British utility company Thames Water, and Canada's energy giant Nexen, to name a few.

There was a time when Westerners assumed the Chinese would convert to Western ways. But China did not become more like us, particularly in regard to business. We voice our misgivings as we count the ever-increasing dots China makes on the world map. That is no matter to China, which will ignore our moralizing about human rights while it continues to buy into Western companies, absorb Western marketing and branding know-how, locate and exploit natural resources, build other countries' infrastructures, and make loans to the deficit-hobbled rest of the world.

Despite China's global importance, its domestic economic growth has not included all of its citizens equally. That can be said about most other nations, but unlike other nations, China has used its position as a world economic leader to fund the solutions to its own problems. It is doing this by identifying strategic partners in countries whose governments welcome China's cash flow and are relieved that China is willing to stay clear of local politics.

For good or for ill, the long-term mission of several emerging markets—Africa, for example—is being shaped by the Chinese. Chinese prisoners are sent to Africa to build infrastructure there so that China has access to the continent's natural resources; and to grow food there, which is shipped back to China.

Some suggest this is bound to have political side effects. Others insist it pits China's state capitalism against fair competition. Speculation on these issues will undoubtedly continue, for it can be accurately said that any attempt to completely understand the Chinese is unlikely. "[The Chinese] are always doing something or saying something that rubs rudely against my hypothesis [of a conception of Chinese character]," wrote George Wingrove Cooke, a China correspondent for the London *Times*. That contentious claim was made in 1857, and there has been little breakthrough in cross-cultural understanding since. But I am unconvinced that China is fomenting a global economic conspiracy in attempting to restore the wealth and power—*fuqiang*—it systematically lost during the last century. China is not sighted on the world's horizon line because it cannot afford to take its eyes off its own profound challenges. The ruling Communist Party seems to me focused primarily on staying in power, and its methods are grounded in functionality.

Despite the speed and scale of China's ascent, failed attempts by foreign companies to monetize China's vast population litter its landscape, and so it is prudent for Western businesspeople to understand that there are two Chinas. China is the world's most dynamic economy, and at the same time it is a developing country where business often veers off course.

Westerners should keep their wits about them to avoid being led into a bog of murky information.

It is not by mistake that it is difficult to parse the significance of official documents. Due diligence—standard in Western countries—is often prevented by Chinese participants with vested interests in suppressing information and the political connections to do so.

Conducting any business in China comes with a learning tax. I paid mine by holding the dimly lit view that business in China thrives on inconsistencies. Had I seen what was squarely in front of me, I would have recognized that, in practice, consistency is reflected in the deference with which the Chinese approach everything.

How one exchanges business cards, for example—and the deference associated with it—often affects the outcome of a business opportunity. In the East, exchanging cards is a surrogate for the Western handshake. Cards appear at every occasion—business or social—even when it is unlikely that you will ever again see the person you are meeting. China's middle managers might be carrying several different cards for the simple reason that it is not at all unusual to hold simultaneous positions in various—and sometimes entirely unrelated—companies.

Having conflated their personal interests with that of the state, senior Chinese executives are committed to one company at a time. They take themselves seriously and expect a show of deference from their Western counterparts, especially when introductions are made. A double-sided Western business card with simplified Chinese on one side is the first indication of respect; its conspicuous absence is not unlike refusing to shake hands at the start of a Western business meeting.

Business cards in China are an extension of the person to whom one is being introduced, so Westerners would be wise to make sure theirs are not only immaculate but are offered in the proper fashion. It is up to the Westerner to present his card first, done with two hands—the card Chinese side up—and facing your contact so he can read it. Even if you are familiar with his title and position, deference is shown by studying the card he has ceremoniously given you and then deliberately placing it within clear sight if you are sitting around a conference table.

Common sense dictates that under no circumstances should you clean your fingernails during a meeting, much less use someone else's business card to do so. Unfortunately, common sense was nowhere to be found when an American colleague used the tip of a business card to dislodge what was under his thumbnail and, in so doing, derailed our chances of a successful outcome.

In all fairness to my countrymen, I cannot claim a faultless record of behavior in China despite my many years of travel there. Cultural misunderstandings have opened up beneath me like sinkholes, and the most fundamental procedures have often resulted in my best and worst impulses overlapping. The rudimentary procedure of a business meeting can invite any number of potential mishaps in the East.

During my meetings with Chinese book editors, the East-West gap declared itself with a matchless range of unrecognizable methods and manners. The first of those meetings was to take place over lunch. I arrived at the designated restaurant at the designated time, which was noon—precisely the time the editor phoned to ask if I was where we had agreed to meet.

"Where the hell else would I be?" I muttered to myself after reassuring him. Of course I would wait for his arrival, I told him. Having rushed to get to the restaurant of his choosing so as not to keep him waiting, I waited the forty minutes it took for him to get there. It was enough time to realize that the Chinese way of doing things was so removed from anything I would ever understand that it hardly seemed worth the effort for me to be outraged.

"Time is money" is the unrelenting warning from Westerners. Inconvenient as it is for them, the definition of time in China does not designate when one hour gives way to the next. Noon, which to me is as definite a time as any other, can be employed by the Chinese as a two-hour period from 11:00 a.m. to 1:00 p.m.

My personal take on time is of little consequence in countries that function with a far less rigorous version of it. Since different cultures interpret time in different ways, I learned that in China it was best to set meetings in the offices of those with whom I intended to meet. My next meeting—with CITIC Publishing Group, whose parent company is China's largest state-owned investment entity—was held in its conference room.

In the West, it is customary to open a meeting with a relatively short introduction and to concentrate on issues that require discussion or decision. The meetings with my potential Chinese publishers evoked a séance-like feeling and were frustratingly nonparticipatory. I later realized that the staff of each had such an extreme reverence for the passively assertive director seated at the head of the table that rarely did anything actually happen. After sitting through these endless, action-deprived meetings, I couldn't begin to guess why they resulted in enthusiastic offers from all four publishers. That didn't prevent me from being delighted, and I chose Xiron Publishing Company, a non-state-owned but state-controlled publishing house run by young and eager managers.

My agent secured a deal in two weeks. I was given three months to complete a guide to Western business etiquette, unaware that I was one of very few Westerners collaborating with a Chinese publisher in order to produce a book exclusively for a Chinese audience. That fact alone was enough to bring me to the attention of the government authorities, who ordered the publisher to scan my visa.

After signing a contract written in Chinese, oblivious to government censors looking over my shoulder, I began to write the kind of book the Xiron editor told me he wanted.

My first chapter, on Western greetings, included instructions on how to shake hands. Though Chinese businessmen do seem to be making the effort to shake hands with foreigners, they offer a weak version that Westerners insist employs too limp a grip. The fact is a limp handshake is regarded in China as an indication of respect; it can be put in perspective when one is reminded that, during imperial times, those who greeted the emperor were expected to kowtow, a gesture of humility that required them to kneel and knock their foreheads on the floor no fewer than nine times.

Kowtowing has since been replaced by *gongshou*—"fist clutching"—a far less humbling ritual of respect saved for traditional festivals and wedding ceremonies, where blessings and well wishes are out in full force. Its staccato-like movements—suddenly stiffened backs and abrupt gesturing with extended elbows and shaken fists—appear to me most appropriate between men.

With her advantage of sexual duality, Phyllis would have been better equipped to identify the gender-related issues of greetings in China. You will appreciate why I did not hold Phyllis up as an example in *The Tao of Improving Your Likability*. I kept my advice simple, with instructions that might just as well have been directed to Western men.

→ *LESSON 1*

A woman need not stand when being introduced, unless that person is much older or she is receiving someone in her office. But a man always rises when a woman comes into the room, and he remains standing until she is seated or leaves his immediate vicinity.

Men, your grip speaks volumes. Limp implies weakness. Too hard comes across as domineering. A medium-firm grip conveys confidence and authority. If you are sitting, stand up and smile. Looking directly at that person shows that you are focused on that one person alone. But don't overdo it. A fixed smile makes you look insincere (because it is). Unblinking eye contact gives the impression that you are possibly dangerous. Repeat the name of the person to whom you are being introduced, as in, "How do you do, Mr. So-and-So." Not only is it flattering, it helps you remember his name.

→ *LESSON 2*

At one time or another, most of us have been introduced by a wrong name or with a misleading identification. The person being incorrectly introduced should correct the error, but in a way that does not bring awkwardness.

Americans are often willing to forfeit manners for convenience, and—with their bone-crushingly enthusiastic handshakes—they seem to be most comfortable when they are at their least formal. In other countries, informality is not necessarily considered a virtue; indeed, it is often seen as a sign of disrespect. An analogous lesson for Westerners in China would be not to address people by their first names unless they have made a point of asking you to do so.

I am guilty of elaborate mistakes with people's names. Chinese names, in particular, are targets of my relentless assault, so I have learned to ask for help pronouncing them. I am also easily confused by given and family names. In Asian countries, including China, the order is reversed, with the family name first. Though more and more Chinese are using their chosen English names when dealing with Westerners, an appreciated course of action is to ask which name the person prefers.

→ *LESSON 3*

Don't worry about making mistakes when introducing one person to another. What's important is that you make the introduction, for it is a breach of manners *not* to introduce two people in your presence who don't know each other. Give both names of both people who are being introduced, regardless of their rank in a business setting. First-name introductions should occur only with children. You should always look first at the person to whom you are making the introduction, then turn to the person you are presenting. There is considerable variation in what to say when making the introduction, but the basic points are that a younger person is presented *to* an older person and that a man is presented *to* a woman, even if he is an older man and she is a young woman. Silence should not follow an introduction. An agreeable "A pleasure to meet you" will suffice.

CHAPTER FIVE

As soon as I finished writing the first chapter of my book, it was translated into Chinese.

The Chinese editor responded quickly in two ways: he returned my manuscript pages marked with editorial notes in Chinese, and he requested that the entirety of my passport be scanned.

"They've already scanned my visa—why scan every page of my passport?" I wondered out loud.

"That's the way they operate," Gilliam said.

"Who is 'they,' and what could they possibly be worried about?" I asked. "It's a book about manners."

"You'll be hauled off by the authorities and never know why. Like the doomed Kafka character in *The Trial*," Gilliam said in jest.

"Well, before I'm hauled off, make yourself helpful and translate what the editor has written in his margin notes," I told Gilliam.

He read the editor's notes and chuckled.

"What's so funny?" I asked.

"It has to do with hygiene. They want to make sure you instruct the reader to wash his hands before shaking other people's hands so he doesn't 'bring his own dirt.'"

After considering the editor's request from a Chinese perspective, I realized he was absolutely right to emphasize the basics.

To a Westerner, it would be an understatement to say men's grooming in China appears casual. While living in Dongzhimen, I managed to acclimate to the jarring display of male nipples and bellies—a visually unpleasant result of the practice of men rolling their T-shirts above their chests to cool down—but what took its daily toll on me was the guttural sound of hawking that would precede spitting . . . and the profuse evidence of it on the streets. The low-water mark came, literally, in the middle of a business meeting when the man sitting next to me pulled the ashtray closer so he could spit in it—a transgression beyond all reasonable bounds that prompted me to include an emphatic "never" in my second chapter.

→ **LESSON 4**

Never spit in front of a Westerner or when traveling outside of China. Wash your hair often enough to keep it from looking greasy. Take a shower daily to avoid body odor, and avoid using too much cologne or cologne that has too strong a smell.

With further thought, I added, "Anything that requires clipping should be done in the bathroom, preferably yours." It was the same suggestion I'd made twenty years ago to a man in New York.

"I usually do that at home, in my bathroom," I told the man sitting next to me on the subway after he pulled something from his coat pocket, crossed one leg over his knee, removed his shoe, pulled off his sock, and proceeded to clip his toenails.

"Give me one good reason I should, bitch," was his very New York response.

No woman likes to be called a bitch, despite the fact that each of us—at one time or another, in a variety of ways—has invited that accusation.

In what was a public setting, I decided not to give the man's name for me any obvious credence. Repressed anger curled the edges of my words, and the suggestion I offered was only slightly bitchy.

"Well, if you look at my lap, where your toenail clippings seem to be landing, we can count the reasons together."

My suggestion was ignored, but remained relevant when, waiting early one morning in the Cathay Pacific lounge at the Hong Kong airport, I heard the same distinct sound of clippers at work.

It cannot be, I told myself before turning around.

A man in a business suit had removed his right shoe and sock to concentrate on the decidedly private task of clipping his toenails. I need not belabor my dismay, but I will take the liberty of stating that this particular lapse in judgment seems to have nothing whatsoever to do with socioeconomic differences or cultural divides. It is, instead, a gender-specific failure of comportment.

Generalizations made by one sex about the other are almost always unfair and often wrong. But I think most would agree that, regardless of the cultural standards by which men have been brought up, they seem capable of ignoring personal hygiene when left to their own devices. That unhappy fact inevitably results in discomfort for others, especially those sharing a confined space such as an office.

WITH VARIOUS ISSUES of personal hygiene put to rest in the second chapter of my book, it seemed logical that the third chapter should cover the topics of posture and clothes. I considered what my mother might have advised, for despite the fact that she was mentally ill, my mother was often right. She believed that when personal appearances were left unattended, they had an ill-fated habit of moving perception to unattractive reality.

"What do you intend to wear?" had been her only question when I was unexpectedly subpoenaed by the Federal District Court in Manhattan on a troubling professional matter.

I tried explaining the grave situation.

"I've spent the entire weekend reading legal briefs," I told her. "What I wear to court can't possibly matter."

"It matters a great deal," she said. "First impressions set the tone, so I suggest a simple ensemble in brown—it's a serious color but not severe. And, dear, please take this in the spirit in which it's given: your height sometimes makes it look as if you're looming. Adding gratuitous inches with high heels will only make matters worse. Be sure to wear flats."

Chinese women have experienced as many dramatic changes in fashion as China has experienced changes in its culture. Until the early twentieth century, when the painful practice of binding the feet of young girls in China came to an end, wealthy husbands displayed their wives' tiny shoes as a sign of proud possession. Social class and custom determined women's outward presentation before the 1950s. In the 1960s, "Mao green" clothing became the norm. Subdued blue and gray were allowed a uniformed appearance in the 1970s. Women remained androgynously indistinguishable from men until the 1980s, when they were granted options of what to do for a living.

Observations from living in Beijing were that mainland Chinese women dress predominantly in copies of Hong Kong fashions, some more successfully realized than others; that bright colors are preferred; and that hair—that disproportionately important issue with women, no matter their nationality or age—has managed to express individual style statements in the way it is cut, colored, or permed.

The decree of fashion is almost always arbitrary, but—like a self-fulfilling prophecy—good or bad posture creates the impression you leave with others, and so my lesson on advisable attire for Chinese businesswomen began with the subject of posture.

→ *LESSON 5*

Standing up straight makes you appear more confident.
If you put your shoulders back while walking and

standing, you will give the illusion of being taller and slimmer. Conversely, if you slouch, you tend to look older, discouraged, and tired. When you sit in a chair, don't fall into it; lower yourself gently. When seated, don't slump. You seem smarter and more alert if you sit up straight.

Clothing should fit properly. Keep jewelry to a minimum. Avoid earrings and bracelets that dangle: both are more appropriate after business hours. Handbags and tote bags should be clean and should complement your outfit. Shoes can be comfortable but should not have worn-down heels or scuffed tips and should be polished. Hands and nails must be well taken care of—no chipped polish—and when wearing open-toe shoes, you should have pedicures frequently. No visible lingerie; no snags or runs in your stockings. Use as little makeup as possible. Finally, your hair should never get in the way.

Hair seems to have been a flash point in my business life. At one time, my hair was an abundant mass of Pre-Raphaelite waves that distracted male colleagues, including the man to whom I reported at Hearst. After managing eye contact during my first debriefing, he turned around and walked into the wall. That incident convinced me to wear my hair pulled back at work.

Hair is but one example of the self-restraint required by business. Indeed, a Confucian approach is just as relevant in the West as it is in the East: regardless of gender, dressing appropriately in the office means toning down one's individual look out of regard for others.

→ *LESSON 6*

For men, conservatively cut dark suits (gray, brown, or navy blue) are best for the office. Wear pale shirts and inconspicuous neckties and socks. Make sure your shirttail is not out and there are no stains on your tie. Polish your shoes and press your clothes each day. Baseball caps are not appropriate attire in a business setting. Leave the backpack at home. Do not wear sunglasses indoors.

My friends from L.A. are different from those in other places. They wear sunglasses indoors. Most of them are in the entertainment industry, and so they have more disposable income and are better-looking than the rest of us. When I was exchanging plans for the holidays with a group of them over dinner, I mentioned that Gilliam—thirteen at the time—wanted a cloak as a Christmas present.

"Where the hell did he get that idea?" asked one in the group.

"Probably from reading too much Sherlock Holmes," was my guess.

"A cloak has style," said another in the group, an artist. "Not everyone could pull it off. It shows confidence."

"He'll be ridiculed by his classmates," said the man's wife, a well-known performer. She was quick to point out that, like her daughter, Gilliam was an only child who had grown up surrounded with adults. It was crucial that he learn to live among those in his age group, she said. Better he not call too much attention to his unconventional tendencies.

The woman urging me to remain sartorially on message was someone I knew from the years I lived in L.A., but not for the reason she was known to the public . . . until that fall, when I saw her sitting on a crescent moon lowered onto a Broadway stage in New York.

It was a dazzling performance. I followed her husband to her dressing room to tell her so. Rows of tassels—circumnavigating all aspects of her blindingly spangled costume—had only recently come to rest after swirling through the last song she'd belted out while dancing in front of a chorus line of deliberately gay-looking sailors. That she was wearing a hat in the shape of an aircraft carrier didn't mitigate her concern that Gilliam might be making a wrong choice in attire.

→ *LESSON 7*

You will never go wrong if you wear appropriate clothes for the occasion. Man or woman, being well-dressed is the result of asking yourself: *Where will I be today (or tonight)? What will I be doing? Who is it I am meeting?*

CHAPTER SIX

Before doling out advice on topics more complicated than shaking hands and proper grooming, I thought it would be wise to understand China's perception of itself.

Any preconceived notion of China by the West is a falsification, for China is infinitely more complex a place than can be imagined. And since the Chinese people take their cues from their government, a better understanding of China's government seemed a logical place for me to start.

A diagram of China's governing bodies has the strangely reassuring look of a corporate management chart. The almost three-thousand-member National People's Congress elects the Central Committee of some three hundred. The Central Committee selects an elite council of twenty-five, the Politburo. The Politburo nominates the Standing Committee, the innermost core of the Chinese Communist Party's power, currently consisting of seven members. Each has a portfolio covering a major area of concern, including the economy, internal security, and propaganda. It is believed that the Standing Committee, led by the president and general secretary, meets once a week and that its decisions are made by consensus.

Though the Communist Party has a precisely defined hierarchy, it functions within an oblique decision-making process, one that strengthens the conviction among Westerners that there is an over-catheterized relationship between China's policymakers and its business leaders. Westerners are right in their belief, for not only do China's state-orchestrated policies subsidize Chinese companies, but the very regulators who arbitrate business approvals and contracts in China are often conducting business within the same sector they are meant to be regulating.

Having learned costly lessons from the disastrous decisions made unilaterally by Mao, the party has since ensured that no single leader be in a position to arbitrarily push through his own agenda. Despite the fact that the top of its governmental pyramid can be depicted by a streamlined flowchart, at its base, China is a collection of decentralized municipalities forming a massive political organism. The Standing Committee sets direction, but it leaves the implementation of policy to the party's bureaucratic apparatus. Policy approval requires the right stamp—and I do not mean this in the figurative sense. Those wielding power within the labyrinthine administrative systems hold stamps of approval that are kept in tightly guarded safes.

The size of the Chinese bureaucracy and the kinds of contradictory edicts it issues often send bolts of panic through foreign investors. China's policies—by Western standards heavy-handed and often coming out of the blue—are considered routine realignments in China.

Sixty-five years ago, the People's Bank of China became the nation's major operating bank. It reported directly to the central government, and its city branches acted as both a central and a retail bank for the entire country. Though commercial functions for the Bank of China were transferred to other state-owned banks in the 1980s, its clout remained squarely in place, the result of broad monetary policies granted to it by the central government on the all-important issue of liquidity—a liquidity that fed growth on the municipal level and, until recently, relied on relatively little debt.

Like most foreign businesspeople eyeing China's growth—which averaged some 10.5 percent when I arrived in the country—I envisioned large multiplications. And like most foreign businesspeople, I failed during my early years of attempting to do business there to sufficiently take into account that the country's government and its businesses are conjoined.

So extensive is the relationship between executives and government officials that it is not uncommon for the latter to claim a part of the assets of the former. My business dealings progressed only when I abandoned my blind adherence to a Western perspective and acknowledged the reasons it was not unusual for the CEO of the state-owned firm with which I was dealing to also hold a ministerial rank in the party. Within that context, the high level of respect China's government officials command from its business leaders remains a pervasive indication of the Confucian principle of top-down control of "leader and subject." It also illustrates the jigsaw puzzle aspect of the country's localized authority.

To mitigate my financial worries while writing my book in China that summer, I took on some consultancy work. One of my clients was a successful Chinese businessman for whom I arranged a meeting with the CEO of a French company. At first, the meeting went well—both parties exchanged information and pleasantries—and everything seemed to be progressing smoothly. But in the middle of the French CEO's presentation, the Chinese businessman's cell phone rang. He took the call. The phone conversation went on long enough for the French CEO to feel he was being insulted.

Afterward, I talked to the Chinese businessman and politely asked him what he was thinking. He explained that the call was from a local government official who—though in a minor position—was considered a higher priority, far more important than the possibility of a relationship with the French CEO. Someone as successful in business as I was, he suggested, must surely have learned how to demonstrate the proper respect to my superiors? His rhetorical question underscored a fundamental but recurring misunderstanding between Chinese and Western businesspeople: both might well be bowing in deference, but not necessarily in the same direction.

———

WHILE AMERICANS ARE eager for independence in virtually everything they do, the Chinese have been instilled with humility. Deference—no matter its cultural provenance—demands outward observance. And despite my often-vocalized opinions, I long ago learned to demonstrate the appropriate level of deference to those to whom I reported.

A business not thought of as entirely businesslike in the 1970s, book publishing granted itself an extremely relaxed attitude toward the issue of hierarchy and provided me with a rapid rise up the ranks to become the head of a company at twenty-nine.

My age seemed to have made it easier to forgive my gender. It was as though one improbability canceled out the other and became a reassurance to my male colleagues that I was more anomaly than threat.

Authors are a mercurial lot who do not take to casual interlopers. With no real experience but a great deal of determination, I began to build my professional relationships on trust. Trust was made easier by demonstrative traits of empathy and consideration—etiquette by any other name—deployed especially when it came to the older men with whom I worked.

Rather than meeting in my office to confront Anthony Burgess about his overdue manuscript—and knowing how much music meant to him—I took him to a jazz club to hear Mel Tormé and persevered the next day. After successfully bidding on Richard Nixon's book—but sensing he would be uncomfortable with all that I appeared to be—I asked the company's older and extremely Republican-looking editorial director to attend the introductory meeting.

And so it went. Comportment took an early lead in my career. What held the middle distance was an increasingly mature sense of when to stand my ground and when to defer. Along the way, I learned not to allow my personal grievances to hinder progress. I also learned that the only thing a man likes less than being wrong is hearing that he is wrong from a woman. My managerial approach invited collaboration, but I was bluntly direct in expressing what needed to happen on behalf of the profit margins. When the dailiness of being surrounded with a male staff threatened my sanity, what restored reason proved to be a decidedly female trait: patience.

Committed to succeed, I worked through my twenties without stopping, until the preconceived notions about my age and gender became secondary to my accomplishments. Only then did it dawn on me that, as a businesswoman, I was at my most effective when I knew enough to let go.

Strangely, that realization did not occur in the office.

It came to me in Africa.

CHAPTER SEVEN

You have no business going there," warned Candida.

I offered no defense.

"Of all places, why Rwanda?" she asked.

"To track mountain gorillas," I told her.

"You're kidding," was her reaction.

I didn't answer.

"Well, you've obviously made up your mind, so take some-one who knows what they're doing and go," said Candida. "Have your adventure. Africa is the one place I'd liked to have seen."

"When do we leave?" asked my brother.

My older brother had a history of traveling as only a man could: alone and to remote places. After laborious research—and without the modern-day benefit of the Internet—we man-aged to locate a British safari company willing to coordinate the logistics. At the time we planned the trip, there were fewer than four hundred mountain gorillas. The safari company couldn't guarantee a sighting, but agreed to drive us across Tanzania and make arrangements with the local trackers to lead us into the rain forest.

Foraging mountain gorillas were known to cross from Rwanda into what was then called Zaire. To make matters more complicated, there was an armed rebellion in the Kiva Province of Zaire.

"That's the least of it," warned my brother, sitting across from me at a restaurant table. He'd come to New York the week before our trip; we were discussing our plans over lunch.

"What do you mean, that's the least of it?" I asked. "I can't imagine anything outperforming abduction or murder."

"Schistosomiasis," he replied.

Schistosomiasis is a disease caused by the minute eggs from an insidious parasite, he explained. Streams and lakes in Africa are often contaminated.

"No need to delve into just how the eggs get into the water. Suffice it to say it has to do with a lack of sanitation," said he between mouthfuls.

"The eggs hatch on contact with the fresh water. The free swimming parasites infect snails and emerge as larvae. And, here's the thing . . . the larvae move in the direction of isolated motion—for example, a person wadding in the stream. What's even more remarkable is that they're stimulated by chemicals found in human skin. They enter through the skin's pores and migrate to the liver where they develop a kind of oral sucker in order to feed from red blood cells and become worms. The worms produce eggs that pass through the bladder . . . and a next generation of parasites is eliminated into the fresh water by their host."

I stared at him with disbelief. My hand—frozen in midair—held one-half of a tuna salad sandwich.

"Too much information?" he asked me.

"No, no . . . Listen, I can't thank you enough for your thorough explanation," I said sarcastically. "I'm especially pleased to have heard the details during my meal."

"It's not as bad as it sounds," he suggested. "Neither the worms nor their eggs have been found in the brain or spinal cord."

"What proof is there of that?" I asked.

"Autopsies," he said without a trace of concern.

"Wonderful. *Very* reassuring," I said. "Have you considered the fact that autopsies are fairly strong indications that deaths were involved at some point?"

"Listen, Eden, this trip isn't going to work unless you change your attitude," suggested my brother.

The nurse at the Centers for Disease Control was all about efficiency. She reached for a clipboard, affixed a single-spaced sheet of diseases, and—after reading the travel itinerary I handed her—began to check off an unsettling number of the little blank boxes: yellow fever, typhoid, poliomyelitis, tetanus, hepatitis A and B, meningitis, and rabies.

"Are you a journalist?" asked the doctor as he was preparing to put me through the series of vaccinations.

"No," I told him.

"I don't understand," he said, unsheathing the first syringe. "Let's start with your right arm and we'll switch to the other halfway. Why Rwanda? It's a dangerous place—especially now."

"I'm tracking mountain gorillas."

"So, you're a scientist. . . ."

"No." I winced with the second injection.

"Sorry. . . . A researcher?"

"No."

"Let's have that one." He pointed to my other arm. "I don't understand," he repeated.

I explained that I was tracking gorillas for no reason other than to track gorillas. The doctor pointed his syringe up, like someone who'd decided to hold off firing a pistol. The cotton ball he held in his other hand began to ooze alcohol.

"One last question," he said with professional calm. *"Are you mad?"*

"No, I am not mad," I said in a deliberately level voice.

We stared at each other. Silence took on implication, and I thought it best to say something else, something that would make me sound self-aware but not overly defensive.

"Under the circumstances, I suppose denying it might be reason enough to believe I am."

It was a fair statement, all things being equal. His furrowed expression relaxed. "Well, at least protect yourself from the sun. . . . Jesus, look at your skin. You'll burn up," he warned as he swabbed my arm for a final inoculation. "And whatever you do, don't go anywhere near the lakes."

"WHAT ABOUT YOUR hair?"

It seemed a strange reaction when I informed my direct report at Hearst where I was going for the two weeks I planned to be out of the office.

"He made my hair sound hazardous," I told my brother while we packed our supplies.

"I don't think it's your hair per se," suggested my brother as he rolled his sleeping bag into an airless tube. "It's more about the consequences of your hair."

"What the hell does that mean?"

"Well . . . you have to admit you have a lot of it. And then there's the color: it might be the first time the locals have seen a redhead. Your hair could be a magnet for unforeseen trouble."

"Don't be absurd," I said dismissively.

From London, we flew to Dar es Salaam, where, in the late hours of night, we connected with another flight—an antiquated twin-engine plane—to Arusha, also in Tanzania. As soon as I stepped off the plane's rickety stairs into pitch dark, something happened. Something unforeseen.

Hurling itself kamikaze-style from out of nowhere, a gigantic bat dove straight into my hair, which had been piled loosely into a bun. The impact of its plunge produced such a head-snapping jolt that I lost my balance and fell backward. It took two people on the tarmac—one holding me down, the other disengaging the bat from its snarled confusion—to rescue me from what would be the first in a series of unexpected encounters my hair would have with African nature.

Crossing Tanzania by jeep the next day was anything but comfortable. By the time we put up the tent that night, I was numb with exhaustion; after maneuvering myself into my sleeping bag, I let out enough of a sigh for my brother to ask if I was already regretting the trip.

Not at all, I said. Granted, the prehistoric-size bat intent on nesting in my hair wasn't a particularly welcoming greeting. Still, I was very much looking forward to the following day and our drive across the Maswa Game Reserve.

"We're leaving early," said my brother. "We should get some sleep."

"Can you shut off the light," I asked.

The request produced a benign chuckle from my tentmate.

"What's so funny?"

"That's the moon, city girl."

When I woke the next day, dirty from the previous, the guide informed us there was water enough to drink, but not to bathe.

I had a choice: I could remain in a state of suspended panic, or I could brush my teeth with the single swig of water allotted to me that morning and get on with the day. *You're not the point,* echoed the vastness beyond where I stood, and it occurred to me that to insist remote Africa should comply with my urban version of convenience was not only futile but showed an inexcusable prudishness on my part.

Gorillas forage in the upper regions of Rwanda's Virunga Mountains. By the time we got to the mountains' base, it had been three days and nights since my clothes had been dry, ten days since I had bathed, and eleven days since my digestive system had cooperated. Continuing on foot, we hiked up a misted area known for its seventy-two inches of annual rainfall. During our eight-thousand-foot ascent, the temperature dropped in cold, wet degrees.

Our guide explained what to do and—more important— what not to do in the company of gorillas. He instructed us to remain sitting on the ground and not to, under any circumstances, stand upright. He warned us that direct eye contact is considered a threat by the silverback, the dominant male identified by his mammoth size and silver-colored back. We were told that if the silverback approached, we were to bow our heads as a gesture of supplication. Lastly, the guide advised us that if the silverback charged, we were not to run away.

"That's the most idiotic thing I've heard," was my reaction to the guide's instructions. "Of course you run. What's the alternative? To stand your ground against four hundred pounds of charging gorilla? Another thing, I'm not wild about the idea of bowing my head."

"You need to understand something," my brother made clear. "I won't be throwing myself between you and an outraged silverback, so if you have a problem bowing your head for a gorilla, you better come to terms with it now."

"Okay, all right . . . I'll bow my head," I shot back. "But I want you to keep this to yourself. I mean it. If anyone I work with hears this, my credibility goes out the window."

After we'd threaded our way through choking vegetation for two hours, the guide suddenly motioned to us to sit. We sat perfectly still while curiosity overcame the gorillas' wariness of us. Eventually, they approached separately. The younger males first, then several mothers with babies on their backs. All congregated within a few feet.

All but one.

In an unchallenged position on a fallen tree trunk a few yards away was the majestically massive silverback. His penetrating black eyes monitored our slightest twitch. In deference to him—demonstrating a concept that is the mainspring of Confucian belief—I bowed my head and cast my eyes to the ground. Deciding that I was of no consequence, he began to lumber off in the opposite direction. He stopped, turned around, and checked us one last time, presumably to make sure our eyes were still averted.

The hike down the mountain was followed by a cramped jeep ride to Lake Victoria. I was grateful to run on its beach. When I stopped to scan the shoreline, my focus gradually moved from the coast to the gleaming water, transparent down to the lake's smooth, sandy bottom.

It was forbidden.

I knew that.

Hadn't my brother given me the gruesome details? And the doctor . . . hadn't he warned that African lakes were lethal?

Schistosomiasis was a veritable flash card for an unforgettably awful disease.

I am a reasonable person. And so I had a moment of reason, a moment of saying to myself, *Let's not do this.*

I am a reasonable person. But if one takes away those moments of unreason, one has taken away a great many of life's joys.

It might have been because I was on an endless beach without anyone in sight. Perhaps it was the rhythmic sound of lapping waves, or my overwhelming desire to float. Regardless of the reason, I knew exactly what I was doing as I stripped off my clothes and calmly walked into the lake. I submerged myself for as long as breath allowed, then propelled myself to the water's surface and floated in something as close to nirvana as I will ever get.

To eliminate the evidence of my swim, I walked back to the tent at deliberate leisure so my hair was given its chance to dry. Along the way, I found a keepsake from Africa: a shell the moss-green color of its mountains.

By the time we checked into the hotel in Kilimanjaro, the idea of a warm bath had acquired a certain magnitude. Before easing myself into the tub, I caught sight of my reflection in the mirror. Scratched arms and bruised legs testified to what I had put myself through, and a bleak diet had resulted in weight loss I couldn't afford. What was left was a battered wreck.

CHAPTER EIGHT

When I returned from Africa, my mother told me I needed my head examined.

She was phoning from a mental institution.

"You should have known better," she repeated after I admitted that the altitude sickness I suffered in Rwanda had mutated into pleurisy by the time I saw a doctor in New York.

My European mother was from a different era. She believed men should be managed in a way that prevented them from feeling anything other than taken care of. But she also expected them to assume a leadership role when the situation required. Apparently, this had been one of those times.

"What possessed your brother to allow you to climb an extinct volcano?" was the rhetorical question she posed before asking a personal one.

"Do you realize how difficult you're becoming to marry off?"

Shengnu, or "leftover woman," is a term China's Ministry of Education has added to its official lexicon. It describes an urban professional woman over the age of twenty-seven. For those slow in understanding the implications, the prefix *sheng* is the same as in the word *shengcai,* or "leftover food."

Setting its own action-oriented time line that delineates exactly when women become stale, the Communist Party provides instruction by age groups. At twenty-five, women must "fight" and "hunt" for a partner. If not married by twenty-eight, women are pressured to "triumph against the odds." Between thirty-one and thirty-four, still-unmarried women are referred to as "advanced leftovers," and by thirty-five, a single woman is the "ultimate" leftover, spiritually flawed in thinking she is higher than the mandate of marriage. That being the case, Li Ping, a young woman I came to admire in Beijing, was spiritually flawed.

Ping was a decent, well-educated, hardworking woman who had made a fortune launching a portfolio of magazines. She had proved herself an astute businesswoman and, by all Western accounts, a great success, but during a revealing conversation in the backseat of her chauffeur-driven Mercedes, Ping told me that her younger sister was more successful in the "important way."

"Why would you think that?" I asked.

"It's not what I think, it's what I know. My sister is married, and I am not. I am shaming my parents."

Ping's punishing words spoke of the worst kind of self-judgment, and, at the time, it was difficult for me to understand the irrational degree to which she was holding her self-esteem in abeyance until she was married.

Fifty years after committing to advance gender equality in China, the Communist Party continues to underestimate the resistance from its nation's culture, a culture that remains rooted in a traditionally Confucian society of male superiority. Only after living in China did I understand how women there struggle to break through the encased male-dominated work environment, not just in circumstantial ways but in the far more complex ways that have to do with self-belief. Very few possess the emotional and financial resources required to brave the tide of political, social, and parental waves pushing them toward marriage.

Ping's plight was not without claims on my sympathy. At one time, I, too, would have been an "advanced leftover." To the surprise of many—myself included—I did marry. Not because my shelf life was just about to expire, but because a man I met (I shall name him W. in this book) was the irresistible contraband the Fates brought on board: charmingly out of order, provocatively incorrect, someone who, from the very beginning, was such good fun it would have been a sin not to have joined him for the rest of my life.

The Chinese character for the word "etiquette" is the same as for the word "custom." It is customary for the groom's family to hire a matchmaker to broker a proposal to the bride's family. If the selected girl and her parents find the proposal acceptable, research is required before the wedding date can be set. Auspicious days for a wedding are subject to interpretation by fortune-tellers, who consult the Chinese almanac—sold at the beginning of the Lunar New Year by street vendors and in bookstores—and perform an analysis based on the bride's and groom's birth dates and hours. Even-numbered months and dates are desirable; the seventh lunar month—the month of the Hungry Ghosts—is avoided. At the time of the betrothal, the groom's family presents the bride's family with gifts that symbolize prosperity, and the bride's parents bestow a dowry on her. Unlike in the West, the Chinese do not exchange wedding vows; rather, they pay their respect to deceased ancestors and the elders in both families. Wedding gifts are in the form of monetary contributions presented in red envelopes.

My own trip down the aisle was not as formulaic.

I was introduced to W. in New York, and our first date was in Paris. Three days later, while I was in Berlin, he phoned from London to propose another chance to see one another when we returned to New York. Our engagement would span ten peripatetic months before we were married in Peru by the captain of a small supply boat carrying us down the Amazon River.

W. spoke Spanish and Portuguese; both came into play during our simple wedding ceremony on the foredeck. That I didn't understand a word in either language seemed inconsequential to everyone but me.

"I haven't a clue what I'm putting my name to," I said, adding my signature to the bottom of the handwritten marriage document.

Signing an agreement in a language I couldn't read was a cavalier conclusion to a day that already had raised questions.

That afternoon, we had taken a walk along the riverbank and met a man who invited us to his nearby hut. Constructed with woven reeds and resting on stilts to accommodate the river's high tide, it consisted of a single room with a roof but no walls.

In spite of what others might consider a privacy issue, the hut was home to the man, his wife, and his daughter, along with his mother and mother-in-law. The household also included a female guinea fowl that, at low water, patrolled the small area under the hut with the territorial aggression of a pit bull. I noticed several pigs; I gathered that they, too, shared the hut when the river rose.

W. conversed with the man, who was obviously delighted to have the male company.

"I think it's safe to say that, in this part of the world, marriage is weighted in favor of the husband," said mine-to-be as we returned to the docked boat.

"What did you two talk about?"

"First of all, the young girl is not his daughter—she's another wife."

"You mean someone else's wife? She looks terribly young for that."

"No, I mean she's his other wife. A second wife. It seems he traded one of his pigs for her. To make matters even more amusing, the pigs were the original wife's dowry."

"I don't find that at all amusing," I said.

"My dear, not only is it amusing, it's a tribute to ingenuity. And did any one of them look unhappy to you?"

I had to admit they did not. Not only were they happy, they were the most civilized people I had ever met.

PART THREE

The Dichotomy
of Personal and Public

行窃的狐狸不出声.

A fox barks not when he would steal the lamb.
—*Chinese proverb*

CHAPTER NINE

Leery of providing the corporate officer to whom I reported reason to believe my professional commitment would be diluted, I withheld the news of my marriage.

A year later, the same executive was deliberately kept unaware of my pregnancy until it became obvious. But attitudes in business change over time and with geographical location.

There has always been a cultural disconnect between the two biggest U.S. coastal cities, condescending New York making self-invented Los Angeles defensive. I was a devoted New Yorker who never lingered longer than a week at a time during my infrequent visits to Los Angeles. I had a respectable career in book publishing, had absolutely no experience in the magazine business, and had never before raised capital. Ignoring both the bleak statistics on the failures of new magazines and the risk-averse premise of impending motherhood, I decided to launch a magazine in Los Angeles. In other words, I made the deeply insane decision to leave a business I understood and start another from scratch in an industry about which I was completely ignorant and in a city I didn't know.

Why I did this, I could not tell you, but I was willing to accept the responsibility for my decision and held stubbornly to it.

With a husband who was a walking definition of the word "freelance" and a baby on the way, I relinquished the security of employment. I would either successfully secure funding for the magazine or go through my limited savings trying.

W. was a cartoonist for *The New Yorker,* and his cartoons became the currency that paid for consultants I couldn't compensate in cash. I took on two partners: an editor and a publisher.

Chance was not unkind.

A fateful seating assignment on a flight the magazine's publisher took to San Francisco got us to what was next. She'd been bumped up to business class. Sitting beside her was Larry Ellison, the billionaire founder of Oracle, who would become our primary investor. With two more investors, there was enough seed money to launch the magazine.

Living as I have in so many places, I've come to the conclusion that a geographical environment has a marked effect on the emotional and psychological characteristics of its inhabitants and, thus, on their social customs. L.A. resides on shifting tectonic plates where the ground has a startling habit of moving. This very well might be the reason people in L.A. operate with a loose interpretation of acceptable behavior.

Unlike my East Coast colleagues, those on the West Coast brought their private lives to the office. Histories of substance abuse were revealed and then revisited during staff meetings, as were details of surrogate birthing options. It wasn't only the office that invited sharing: personal information flowed freely between near strangers. The most staggering example introduced itself at a dinner party when the man seated next to me, late to the table, informed me that he had been in the bathroom checking the color of his urine.

My slack-jawed reaction did nothing to stop him from sharing more.

"Clear urine is a sign my system is prepared to digest another meal," he wanted me to know.

L.A. is a place thought foreign even by its own countrymen. In many ways, life there was my preparation for the eventual experience of living in China. Like people in Hollywood, people in China seem unable to explain what is wrong with what the larger world considers cheating. And both places required me to function in an elliptical state wherein I was never entirely certain about the direction things were heading, especially in business.

In L.A., business lunches give the misguided impression that all at the table are friends who happen to be doing business. In China, people bring strangers to business lunches who have absolutely nothing to do with the business at hand. This might explain why, during the summer I was writing my book in Beijing, I was asked to a lunch with ten people I didn't know.

A Chinese friend had come from New York on business. She is a financier. One of her clients is a major Chinese cell phone company. As a favor to her, I joined the lunch in honor of the company's president. He arrived at the restaurant with a retinue; never more than a foot away was his young, vividly alert vice president. The president spoke no English. The vice president did. He was what is known in China as a *haigui,* or "sea turtle," a young Chinese who comes back to China after being educated in the West.

The lunch conversation unfurled in Chinese, making it difficult to understand if the person who was talking to me was the same person I should be paying attention to. So I sat, smiling and silent, until the end of the meal, when the president said something obviously meant for me.

"Our president has asked if you know Angelina Jolie," translated the young vice president.

The question was hilarious, but I understood enough about *mianzi,* or "saving face," to know that even a fleeting appearance of levity would be a serious mistake.

"No, I'm afraid I don't," were my carefully measured words.

The time it took the young man to translate my answer far exceeded the brevity with which it had been conveyed. Without the benefit of linguistic reference points, I was reduced to watching facial expressions. It looked to me that whatever was being said on the other side of the table had already set in motion circumstances in which my no was not the end of something, but its starting point.

"I understand you lived in Los Angeles," said the young vice president.

"That's right."

"But you don't know Angelina Jolie."

"That's right."

There was more discussion on the other side of the table.

"Do you know anyone who knows her?" asked the vice president.

"Do you?" pressed my friend. "Take time to think," she instructed.

After more thought, I remembered that the producer of one of the actress's earlier movies was an acquaintance from L.A. That obscure piece of information caused a rush of activity. Several at the table made phone calls; others took notes.

"Our president would like you to write your friend and ask him to tell Angelina Jolie that we want her to represent our new smartphone," said the young man. "It comes out next month."

He was serious.

"Well, I'm sorry, but I can't imagine Angelina Jolie would agree to promote a smartphone," I told him. "And in the unlikely event she would, I doubt she's available in the next two weeks."

The silence that followed made obvious that the young man had no intention of translating what I said for fear that his president would lose face. It was my misstep. In the West, candor does the work for honesty; in China, it results in a humiliating loss of face.

My friend suggested that I go to the ladies' room.

"But I don't have to use the ladies' room," I told her.

"Just go," she insisted in an anxious whisper that left no doubt it was what she needed me to do.

I excused myself for the ladies' room, where I waited for a few minutes before returning to the table.

When I took my seat again, my friend told me something that required repeating.

"They'll pay twenty thousand dollars to write the letter."

"*What?*"

"They'll pay twenty thousand dollars to write the letter," said my friend again.

Hearing the absurdity spoken for the second time released my disbelief at having heard it at all.

A riot of thoughts swarmed my head, but the only conclusion I could come to was fairly rudimentary: that something I probably would never understand had happened in the short time I spent in the ladies' room.

"You're looking at me as though I'm suggesting something illegal," said my friend.

"Well, are you?" I asked.

"They're just asking you to write a letter."

"No one is paid twenty thousand dollars just to write a letter."

"In this case, you are."

"Let's say I write the letter. We both know Angelina Jolie won't do it."

"That's not our problem. And on the off chance she can, I've negotiated a percentage of the take."

"You did all of this while I was in the ladies' room?"

"Yes . . . but don't write the letter until they wire the money."

"This is insane. Are you sure I'm not breaking a law?"

"This has nothing to do with the law," my friend pointed out. "This is about *guanxi.*"

How, why, when, and with whom things are done in China depends, on a certain level, upon *guanxi.* Like most idioms, *guanxi* is not easily translated into a single word that mirrors its meaning. "Relationships or connections outside the family" is the closest one might come to the meaning of what is at the very core of Chinese society and culture.

In China, the systematic reciprocity that is *guanxi* produces a never-ending cycle of favors. Among its obligations is to uphold the idea of *mianzi,* or "face." *Mianzi* cements the relationship in place with an acknowledgment of each other's personal dignity—a dignity based on status and prestige.

Even in neocapitalist China, dignity is infinitely more important a commodity than money. Keeping face is paramount; losing it, disastrous; taking it away from someone else, unforgivable. *Any* form of refusal costs face, which is the reason one should not be direct in saying no in China. Conversely, one should never assume that a yes in China is reliable, for the Chinese yes is a transitory, flexible concept.

Since *guanxi* is the tangible result of connections, wealthy Chinese who wish to display their social advancements are increasingly seeking direction on how to entertain Western-ers in their expensive houses. Well and good, but after the host and his guests are seated around the dining table in his home—no matter how expensive—all are expected to know table manners.

CHAPTER TEN

The first book devoted exclusively to table manners was written by Bonvicino da Riva, a Milanese monk, in 1290.

It suggested that "a dinner guest should not blow his nose through his fingers; nor should he scratch himself in any foul part while eating."

Not a bad start. But for most of us, some more direction is needed.

Table etiquette is important to the Chinese. They believe luck is brought with good table manners and shame is the result of bad. Since rudeness can occur without the utterance of a single offensive word, Chinese traditions that govern dining begin with the placement of guests at the table and then address how they are welcomed once they are seated. It remains universally accepted that the most honored position is to the immediate right of the host.

Stationed at the top of ancient China's social pecking order was its imperial court. Next were the grandees and local ministers, followed by members of trade associations. Last—if they made it to the table at all—came the farmers and workers. The post–Cultural Revolution simplification of the four-tier system reduced it to only two: the host and the guest of honor, with the seat of honor reserved for the guest.

Dining tables in China are circular. The lazy Susan—a rotating tray positioned in the center of the table—is employed so that all are an equal distance from the food. The guest of honor starts the meal by serving himself, then turning the lazy Susan clockwise. In a show of hospitality, the host forfeits his place and serves himself last. From the start of the meal until its end, deference is shown to the guest of honor, who is offered the last bite of the most coveted dish on the table.

Imagine, if you can, how bewildering it must be for a Chinese guest at a Western dinner in a private home. Rather than being seated at a round table, which would enable him to observe the other guests, he is flanked with blind spots created by an unyielding, right-angled table. He is expected to know how to help himself with unfamiliar implements to food he cannot identify each time one of the several dinner courses is served by someone who mysteriously appears from behind or to his side.

While writing my chapter on dining for *The Tao of Improving Your Likability,* I put myself in that same lost place of confusion.

→ *LESSON 8*

When you are invited to dinner, immediately inform your host whether you are attending. If you delay your response, you prevent your host from planning ahead. A dinner invitation, once accepted, is a responsibility not to be subsequently subordinated to a better offer. Never ask who else is attending; although the host might volunteer the information, it is not obligatory to do so. Arrive on time, or only slightly late (no more than ten minutes). Do not, however, arrive early. When your host announces it is time for dinner, go straight to the table. If you have not yet met the other guests, introduce yourself to the people sitting near you. There are usually four courses to a Western meal: a first course (customarily soup or an appetizer), a main course, a salad, and a dessert. With the exception of the first course, you are often expected to serve yourself from a platter that is being passed or is placed in front of you. Take a portion closest to you, put the serving fork and spoon back together on the serving platter, and wait for your host to begin before starting to eat.

It must be a relief for the Chinese to know that dining at a Western table is limited typically to four courses. Alas, that cannot be said for a Westerner in China, where the meal begins with a set of cold dishes, followed by various courses of vegetables, even before the soup makes an appearance. Next is meat. Then fish is presented, often served whole and never flipped to its other side, which is an unlucky gesture that symbolizes capsizing a boat. Since protein and vegetables claim a higher nutritional rank, starch is consumed as filler if the diner is still hungry. When bowls of rice and noodles are placed on the table, it usually indicates that the meal is drawing to a conclusion.

Much of social life—and a great deal of business—revolves around food, and I am of the mind that one should know how to behave at the table of people with whom one happens to be dining. Eating in China can be a terror for the uninitiated. At one time or another, I have been immobilized by dishes with ghoulishly unappetizing implications: "pig hoof gruel," "fried goose intestines," "chicken without sexual life," "pockmarked old-lady's tofu," "fish smell like pork," "lover's lung." The real showstopper: "lily bulbs and deer's penis."

Even though I have managed the body parts of both small and large animals, I continue to be outdone by various crustaceans, which appear to require a full set of surgical tools to consume. Not only do I leave the carnage of giant crabs on their serving plate—the unsightly proof of my unsuccessful amputations—but even when I manage to transfer the hacked-up crabmeat onto my plate, I fail to ensure its clear passage to my mouth. A shortcoming with shellfish is but one of my failings at a Chinese table. My mistakes with chopsticks are notorious. I have enlisted them to impale uncooperative food in a last-ditch effort to eat what has been placed in front of me. I have wrongly employed them to pick through the food on my plate, a gesture that represents digging my own grave. And I have used them to pass food, which conjures the passing of cremated bones between loved ones at a funeral. I have left chopsticks sticking out of my rice bowl, a look reminiscent of incense sticks, which burn in veneration of the deceased.

Assisted by my sometimes invincible ignorance of Chinese dining superstitions, I have foretold the impending deaths of everyone at the table and have reminded them of the past deaths of their loved ones. So when it came time for me to offer advice to the Chinese on the fundamentals of Western cutlery, it was my fondest hope that they would succeed where I had so obviously not with chopsticks.

→ *LESSON 9*

A table setting for a four-course Western dinner includes the following:

- Soup bowl
- Dinner plate
- Salad plate
- Dessert plate
- Bread plate with butter knife
- Napkin
- Soupspoon
- Dinner knife
- Dinner fork
- Salad fork
- Dessert fork and spoon
- Coffee spoon
- Water glass
- Wineglass
- Coffee cup and saucer

Utensils are placed in the order of their use, starting from the outside and working in. The exception is the dessert fork and spoon, which are placed above the dinner plate. Forks go to the left of the plate; the knife and the soupspoon go to the right of the plate. The butter knife rests on the bread plate, which goes to the left of the dinner plate. The glasses to the right. One way to remember this: food to the left and liquids to the right.

The ancient Greeks used the fork to hold meat while cutting it. The Italians employed the early use of the fork on its own, but that system failed to win over the English until the late seventeenth century. The dinner knife—which replaced the sharp tip with a rounded one—was not put to daily use until the eighteenth century, when Louis XIV—after discovering its practicality—became an enthusiast. Since its purpose was no longer to prick a piece of food off the plate, but to help with cutting it, the king took advantage of that advancement and banned pointy knives from the dining table.

→ *LESSON 10*

There are two ways of eating in the West: the American way and the Continental way. The Continental way of eating is more streamlined and—to my mind—easier. The fork is held in the left hand and points down. The knife is held in the right hand and low to the plate. They stay exactly that way throughout the meal. The advantage of this method is that you need not constantly pass the fork from your left to your right hand, as you must in the American way. When not cutting, the knife helps guide the food onto the fork. Once you lift your utensils from the table, they stay on your plate and do not go back on the table. Your knife and fork should be put in the resting position on your plate when you raise your napkin to your lips between bites, take a sip of water or wine, or have an extended conversation.

When I lived in L.A., the simple interaction of inviting people to dinner was complicated by their numerous dietary issues. Guests would phone the day before and negotiate the meal, requesting it be dairy-free and reminding me that they don't eat bread after 11:00 a.m.

L.A. is not a reference point for Western normalcy, and so

I alerted my Chinese readers that at most Western tables bread will inevitably be served and is usually passed in a breadbasket.

→ *LESSON 11*

If you are the one who begins to pass the bread, pick up the basket and offer it to the person to your left. After that person takes a piece, help yourself to a single piece, place it on your bread plate (or on the left side of your dinner plate if there is no bread plate), and pass the basket to your right. If you would like butter on your bread, take enough butter from the butter dish to cover the whole piece of bread and put it on your bread plate; never butter your bread directly from the butter dish. Do not take the entire piece of bread to your mouth and leave a dentist's mold of your bite. Break off a bite-size piece of bread from the piece you have placed on your bread plate, and butter each piece as you eat it.

Between what is done at the table is what is said at the table. It is the obligation of the host to make sure his guests are engaged in good conversation, and it is up to the guests to make sure the host does not regret inviting them.

PART FOUR

The Art—and Perils—of Conversing

打人不打脸, 揭人不揭短.

Although there exist many thousands of subjects for elegant conversation, there are persons who cannot meet a cripple without talking about feet.

—Chinese proverb

CHAPTER ELEVEN

At times, there is a mangled charm when the Chinese attempt small talk with Westerners. Their total lack of inhibition is the refreshing opposite of the West's politically correct and often spontaneity-killing approach to conversation.

It turns out that the Chinese are capable of asking what most people want to know but, with the exception of young children, are too polite to ask.

Having been interrogated about my age, how much money I have, and why I was not married, I've come to enjoy the guileless manner by which the Chinese plunge forward in their conversations with me. For other Westerners, however, the Chinese take on social conversation can seem stunningly taboo-free—to the point of causing discomfort. Making matters worse is that in China grinning serves to lessen embarrassment or to deal with awkwardness in a social situation. Such extreme oppositions in comportment collide when the news of misfortune is met with laughter, and the reply to a Western admonishment for such laughter is yet more laughter.

During the course of a banquet I attended with Chinese and American businessmen and their spouses, our Chinese host began an innocuous enough conversation with the woman seated on his left.

"I see you like food," was how he began.

"Well, yes, I suppose I do like food," responded the woman, charmed by what she assumed was his limited English.

"I knew that because you are fat," was what he said next.

Those close enough to hear waited in stunned silence for the consequence.

There was none.

The brutally expressed observation—accurate though it was—would have been a martini-in-the-face insult anywhere other than China, where, it happens, being plump is a sign of prosperity. That might well be, but my chapter on social conversation warned Chinese readers that under no circumstances would a Western woman agree to put her prosperity on a public scale.

→ *LESSON 12*

Mastering the skill of starting a conversation with someone you've just met requires you to listen carefully to the other person, to be observant, and to think before you speak. Being observant means considering the person you are addressing. If you are anxious, you won't be able to think of anything to say in a group. Wait for the right moment and add your own thoughts or observations to the discussion. An opening line that a host may use to start a conversation is "How do you like our city?" One for a guest at a dinner or function is "How do you know our host?"

The advice in my chapter on conversing with Westerners focused more on what not to say, and I was able to use several unforgettable examples from my own dining table.

Some twenty-four years ago, W. organized a dinner party at our New York apartment to celebrate the impending birth of our son. The conversation was a case study in disaster.

"If you described parenthood as a job, no one would take it," was how it began.

The statement was especially unexpected, coming as it did from a mother of two charming children. Of those gathered at the table, her husband was the most taken aback.

"What a discouraging thing to tell someone who's just announced she's expecting!" he said.

Choosing to ignore him, his wife turned to me. "You're a businesswoman, Eden. If you were to list the pros and cons of the theoretical job of being a mother, would there be any takers?"

It was the kind of interrogative that had no intention of waiting for a reply. Before I could answer, her composure snapped like a dry tree branch.

"Even at a six-figure salary, you'd be insane to take the job!" she blurted out.

The unsparing assessment locked us in uneasy quiet.

"It starts with nine uncomfortable months. Each month is its own separate and awful reminder you've lost control of your body. Then there's the backbreaking labor and the searing pain of delivery."

Her evenly spaced words produced the tonal rhythm of a demented storyteller, and our collective expression took a recognizable shape of dismay.

"That's just the beginning," she continued in a monotone flattened by defeat. "You bring home this complete stranger who nurses away whatever strength you have left. By the end of the first month, the novelty has worn thin, just in time to realize your baby isn't an item you've bought and can still return."

She then offered a bleak forecast: "You can be sure of one thing: no matter what you do or how you do it, you know— you just know—that in twenty years he'll be sitting in a psychiatrist's office blaming you for something, some small thing, something you couldn't remember if someone put a gun to your head."

Palpable silence from our other guests failed to camouflage their horror. At the opposite end of the table, my husband's face was telegraphing a wordless plea for intervention.

"So, Cleveland, tell us what you're up to these days," I asked in a transparently obvious bid to redirect the conversation.

Cleveland Amory was a curmudgeon who'd long given up on humans to devote himself to animal rights. To the immediate point, he was someone who had been to enough dinner parties to understand that he was being prevailed upon by a desperate hostess.

"You know how I feel about making fur coats from baby white seals," was his lead-in.

"Yes . . . ?" I said, grateful that he had taken my cue.

"Well, I'm working with the Greenpeace people, and the really good news is we plan to sink a Canadian trawler next week."

The transition to another topic was more abrupt than I might have liked.

"Isn't that dangerous for someone?" I asked.

W. leaned forward in his chair. His keen interest pushed aside my concern about safety in favor of the pyrotechnical details.

"How do you sink something that size? What does it take?"

His was a question only a man would ask and other men would appreciate. I was surprised when the one sitting to my left—Robert, who was both a close friend and our lawyer—stood up suddenly and excused himself.

Cleveland continued to detail his plan. He would implement his scheme at night, when a skeleton crew would be on board; the boat would be anchored in shallow waters; explosives would be limited to a small detonating device in the boiler room.

Robert had been in the bathroom for what I thought was an overly long period of time. After clearing his plate from the table, I discreetly inquired of his wife if she thought her husband was all right.

"He'll come back after the subject changes," she said obliquely.

I tapped on the bathroom door. "Bob?"

"Is he finished?"

"Do you mean Cleveland?"

"Yes."

"With what?"

"With what he was saying."

"I don't know. . . . Why does it matter?"

"Because I can't be witness to a future crime."

"Well, why didn't you say something?"

"It was easier to leave."

"What have you been doing in there all this time?"

"I found my briefcase in the hallway on the way in."

"I'm so sorry," I apologized. "It never occurred to me."

"Is the woman all right?"

"She seems to be . . . but I don't think her marriage will ever be the same."

"Well, tell my wife to come for me when your guests have left."

Robert would not have felt the need to lock himself in the bathroom if all at the table had followed the basic dos and don'ts of polite conversation.

→ *LESSON 13*

Social conversation is a give-and-take. The best occurs naturally. Unfortunately, this is also true with the worst. Stay away from provocative subjects and depressing topics that are liable to paralyze the other guests. Consider the person you are addressing, for it is unlikely that a woman, obviously delighted by her pregnancy, appreciates hearing that her baby will drain the life out of her. Don't interrupt someone who is speaking, no matter how enthusiastic you are about entering the conversation. Avoid preempting the choice of topic, and don't keep to any one subject for too long: it holds the other guests conversationally captive. Don't talk at length about a place or person when it becomes apparent that no one else in your group has been there or knows the person. Don't tell jokes unless they fall within the bounds of good taste, are at no one's expense, and are easily understood by all in the group. It is rude to probe. Rather than pry into anyone's marital status, ask the hostess the next day. Under no circumstances ask questions about a guest's or the host's wealth.

"Are other things considered rude?" scribbled my Chinese editor in his margin notes.

His question led me to contemplate a larger underlying issue: what exactly does it take to live acceptably among other humans? In our own culture, most of us know what is expected; there are standards to follow that drive a consistency of behavior. But how should we behave when we have no idea what constitutes rudeness outside our own cultural arena? One should not slurp soup, nor should one belch at the table. *Who would doubt something so right?* you might ask. But for the Chinese, slurping is acceptable and belching is a compliment to the chef.

No matter the foreign land, acts of kindness rarely require an interpreter. Manners, on the other hand, are the complex representation of human interaction based on the history of a particular culture.

American manners are built on a bedrock of freedom. Davy Crockett, the nineteenth-century folk hero known as the King of the Wild Frontier, took only a few short words for his advice: "If it's right, do it." It went without saying that an American's "right" was inarguable and "it" could be anything.

I am of the opinion that the English—with the exception of their Parliament, which is made up mostly of adults determined to behave like rowdy schoolchildren—are so outwardly polite it often prevents the discovery of their delightfully inward quirks and that self-deprecation is probably the only way for them to cope with their nation's postimperial decline.

Residing on the opposite end of the politeness spectrum are the French, most of whom appear unapologetically rude—the result, I am sure, of the French Revolution, a resounding rejection of powdered manners and, to this day, the cause of the disdainful attitude of virtually every waiter in the country.

Unlike the Chinese, who systematically eliminated manners in the name of equity, the French after their revolution kept alive the memory of manners revered, as well as their unshakable sense of self. There is a unique relationship between the French and everything else, and hundreds of years of giving themselves disproportionate credit for simply being French has made them often unbearable, even to their own kind. I have seen this at close range.

At one point in my young parenthood, we lived a year in Paris. On Gilliam's first day of grade school there, it was necessary for me to register him for a cafeteria pass. I had a good look at the other parents. They were well dressed, haughty, and without the slightest shame for cutting in front of me.

"All they do is crowd in and circle the registration table. What's so difficult about forming a line?" I asked Gilliam.

"It's difficult to form a line if everyone in it believes the line begins with them," was the boy's assessment of both the situation and the nature of being French.

The French might not know how to form an orderly queue, but no one would argue that they have style. That same year we lived in Paris was the first the city levied fines against those who neglected to pick up after their dogs. I watched from my apartment window as a beautifully dressed woman of a certain age, wearing leather gloves that matched the robin-blue color of her Hermès handbag, pulled out a plastic bag and, in a single graceful motion, swooped down on the digestive by-product of her little dog. With impeccable sangfroid, she placed the excrement in her handbag in order to avoid being seen carrying it to the garbage receptacle a short block away.

Well done—but maybe not as far as the Chinese are concerned, for they find it unbearable when a man blows his nose in a handkerchief and returns it to his pocket. Lesser infractions named by the Chinese include whistling, snapping one's fingers, pointing, and insisting on discussing business during a first meal. The ultimate display of rudeness—one that will quickly end a relationship—is to force anyone to lose face.

Painful for the French to acknowledge but nonetheless true is that the history of correct behavior in China precedes anything French. At one time, all nations from the Yellow Sea to the Caspian were tributaries to China. In pursuit of a fuller understanding of the Chinese culture, I've read the translations of some of their classics, written before the Bible by several centuries. Contained in them are rules of behavior numbering no less than three thousand—convincing me that altruism in China is not so much expressions of mind and heart as it is ritualistic reenactment.

Since humanity has proved that consideration does not occur naturally I have to believe that anything that can inspire that admirable characteristic—or assigns responsibly when it goes missing—makes us better beings. As I contemplated this issue, it dawned on me that although China has not embraced the concept of religion in quite the same way as has the West, in bodying forth the spirit of their ancestries, the Chinese have created ceremonies and traditions that serve the same functional purpose as religious belief.

The editor had no interest in my free-floating thoughts on the immortal beliefs of the Chinese people. What he wanted were illustrations of Western rudeness. Making good on his request was simple enough. I needed only to reflect on the behavior of my friends for an inventory of what not to do.

CHAPTER TWELVE

At three months, Gilliam was christened in an Episcopal church on upper Fifth Avenue in New York. This respectable event set off a Wagnerian epic of social mishaps.

It began at the church's altar, where Candida, Gilliam's godmother, vowed to what she called the "Jew-God" that she would provide spiritual sustenance.

"If there is a God," said Robert as we left the church, "this crowd has pushed him to his limit of tolerance."

The group of attendees walked to our apartment a few blocks away for the reception. Gilliam needed a nap after his ceremonial responsibilities. One of the guests suggested that since she wanted to use the phone and the phone was in the room with the crib, she would watch Gilliam until he fell asleep. Having written a heavily reported piece scheduled to run in *The Washington Post* the next day, she spent an hour in the nursery conferring with the paper's fact-checker.

When, finally, it occurred to me to look in on both of them, I found Gilliam happily chewing the no-longer-needed marked-up typescript pages the woman was discarding in his crib. The crib's headboard was a graveyard of Post-its, the result of her methodical approach to answering the fact-checker's queries.

After sending the woman from the nursery, I peeled off the Post-its, waited for Gilliam to go down for his nap, and returned to the front room to find Jonathan locked in ani-mated debate with another guest. Jonathan's cake fork had been lifted off the side of his plate and was waving in the air. It lashed out to make an impassioned point, tearing the veiled hat of a woman standing near.

"Make amends and replace her hat," I said to Jonathan after the damage was done.

"I've done her a favor," he insisted. "She looked like a bee-keeper. And anyway, I'm the least of your problems. You should check out what's happening in the kitchen."

Turning my attention to our small kitchen, I realized it was emitting sobs.

One guest had pulled another aside to report that her unfaithful husband was cheating with a spectacular range of women.

After everyone finally left, my father observed, "I've never met more self-absorbed people."

It was his polite way of saying they were all impolite.

In a metaphorical sea of self-involvement, my friends are often storm-tossed by waves of anxiety. Piled into one room, they evoke the chaos of Géricault's *Raft of the Medusa*. It is also true that my friends were behaving with various degrees of rudeness at my son's christening—which enabled me, years later, to explain Western rudeness to my Chinese publisher by setting benchmarks with examples that measured levels of offense.

→ *LESSON 14*

UNWITTINGLY RUDE BUT FORGIVABLE TO A POINT:
· Poor table manners
· Smoking in someone's home without asking permission first

UNCONSCIOUSLY RUDE BUT RUDE NONETHELESS:
· Spitting or belching
· Asking people about their marriages
· Speaking loudly on a cell phone

· Blocking a busy entrance by standing directly in front of the door while chatting with a friend
· Cutting in line

DELIBERATELY RUDE AND DESERVING OF REBUKE:
· Shouting obscenities at a person
· Calling into question the honesty or capability of a person in front of other people

"So, what should you do when someone is displaying the first or second level of rudeness?" asked the Chinese editor.

My advice might just as well have been offered to Westerners. . . .

→ *LESSON 15*

Being considerate prevents you from being rude. Sadly, it does not prevent others from being rude to you. If you are on the receiving end of bad behavior, consider the situation before reacting, and don't automatically take it personally. Sometimes the offender has had a bad day or is unaware he or she has offended. Take a few breaths and ask yourself if it's worth a confrontation. If you do decide to say something, even about the offense of casual rudeness, keep in mind that how you say what you want or need to say makes all the difference. When correcting an intrusive display of rudeness, better that the tone of your voice should be gentle and not harsh—a challenge for Chinese people, whose nature is to speak louder than most Westerners.

"Okay, but what happens when someone is rude to you at the third level of rudeness?" asked the editor, as if putting us both through a ballistic defense exercise.

"Keeping your dignity after being insulted depends upon how you react," I added to the text. "Nothing is lost by taking the higher ground, and many times the best solution to being insulted is to not confront the person who has been rude."

It was at this point that I had to admit to myself it was easier to write such a thing than to do it.

Each of us has a different threshold of tolerance when it comes to the rudeness of others. I react to rudeness by being a model of politeness myself. This reversed equation of behavior equips me with verbal tools to attack aggressive rudeness with sarcasm and provides me with a benefit of doubt when bearing witness to casual rudeness. I have been known, however, to frighten people when my patience has been entirely expended, especially when it comes to business matters.

It is not much of an exaggeration to say that I am impossibly obstinate when my unyielding determination refuses to listen to reason. But it also must be said that, unattractive as it is in an unvarnished state, tenacity is the thing entrepreneurism is made of. It was my unattractively willful self that enabled me to consider launching a magazine in L.A., never having lived there and with absolutely no experience in magazine publishing.

PART FIVE

The Cost of Doing Business

无奸不商.

He who has never been cheated cannot be
a good businessman.

—*Chinese proverb*

CHAPTER THIRTEEN

Robert deferred his legal bills, which made forming Buzz Inc. possible, and I left New York with barely enough seed money to launch the magazine in L.A.

A year of nonstop work produced impressive results: newsstand sales, subscriptions, and advertising revenue performed better than the figures driving our business model. But in business—as in life—timing can hold success hostage. The day we entered a second stage of financing, the stock market plummeted five hundred points and our funding disappeared. More time was bought by collateralizing ad revenue already committed from the magazine's multi-issue contracts in order to borrow enough money to publish two more issues. Sales continued to climb; still, no funding came.

After months of trying to finance the magazine, I was prepared to give up when we realized we couldn't pay for the rented office furniture anymore. Then the one remaining phone rang. It was an unknown Englishman calling from Bangkok.

"I've been on holiday in Hawaii, where I came across a copy of your magazine," explained the Englishman, who introduced himself by name only.

How on earth did a copy of the magazine end up in Hawaii? I wondered.

"Is the company that owns the magazine private?" asked the Englishman.

"Yes . . . ?" I said, more question than confirmation.

"I represent the proprietor of a major media company based in Bangkok who's looking for investments in the United States, preferably in L.A.," was what the Englishman told me.

THE PRACTICE OF eighteenth-century Thai monarchs to take daughters of wealthy Chinese as concubines created two distinct advantages for the Thais: it established political connections in China, and it encouraged Chinese merchants to infiltrate trading houses in Thailand, which kept the Europeans in line.

Sondhi Limthongkul is a Chinese Thai, which makes him an entrepreneur by nature and design—one who had multiplied a single business publication into thirty more and a personal fortune.

I flew to Bangkok to meet him.

Travel without your family is a different kind of travel. Enrichment comes by what is experienced from what you—and sometimes only you—know of yourself. In fact, some of the best moments in travel lose their moments when, afterward, you are forced to describe them anecdotally to someone else.

No matter how dearly I loved W., he would not have understood my delight the moment I spotted Peter Ustinov walking through the lobby of the Mandarin Oriental in Bangkok. In fact, if W. had been with me, the moment would not have been the same.

It wasn't simply a pleasure of the moment, but rather the personal history of its parts. It had to do with being told by Jonathan that, before leaving Bangkok, I should have lunch at the Mandarin Oriental, where I should make a point of ordering a club sandwich and enjoying the view. He hadn't disclosed what the view would be, allowing me the pleasure of anticipation. It was that the view turned out to be of the magnificent sweep and the constant activity of the Chao Phraya River . . . that the club sandwich rewarded me with a recognizable taste of home . . . that the delicious sandwich, made with perfect toast, was on an elegantly simple white plate, placed on a table draped in crisp white linen. The table was on a terrace outdoors, so I could feel a warm breeze, and it was far enough from the next table that I could imagine I might have been the only one looking out at the world. It had to do with the fact that I was sitting by myself, with myself, but that I also loved my husband and son a world away . . . and that I was part of a family to which I would be returning soon.

The moment also had to do with my mother, a complicated and emotionally unavailable woman, who, for reasons unexplained, had simply stopped talking to me one day the year prior. But before she did—in a fleeting comment—she made herself available enough to tell me she admired the wit of Peter Ustinov, the intellectual acuity of Peter Ustinov, his gift of mimicry and his keen interest in art history. It was that— after the sandwich, the river view, the sublime happiness at my own good fortune—the object of my mother's admiration was walking toward me in the lobby, headed to the pool in a white terry cloth robe and flip-flops.

All the moments became a single, aggregated moment. It suggested itself in his eyes before making its way down to the corners of his mouth. Without either of us breaking stride, just at the point we passed each other, Peter Ustinov and I exchanged a smile.

It was a good omen.

The next day, Sondhi, based in Bangkok, agreed to become the magazine's largest shareholder. And like a contrived twist in the middle of a problematic plot, my salvation came from a stranger in a distant land.

During the nine years we worked together, Sondhi proved Western in his professional behavior—by that I mean he was goal oriented in ways I recognized. But his attitude toward money remained decidedly Asian.

My upbringing had placed the subject of money off-limits, making it difficult for me to discuss it other than in the context of business. Even more uncomfortable for me was the appearance of large amounts of money outside of a bank. And so whenever Sondhi pulled out thick reams of bills from a leather bag handed to him by his assistant, I was not only embarrassed but couldn't help feeling something nefarious was afoot.

Experience is a great leveler, and the longer I conducted business in Asia, the less furtive I felt with the public display of money. By the time I became a consultant in China, I had no problem accepting remuneration in tightly rolled tubes of renminbi and transferring them into Ziploc bags. Like everyone in China, I paid for things in cash. Since the largest bill the Chinese government prints is still the hundred-renminbi note, worth about sixteen dollars, doing and buying things in China takes a great many of them.

Determined to avoid any questions from the IRS, I was scrupulous in reporting my income from China. But—with so much cash changing hands there—I saw how Chinese businesses hid profits in plain sight. It's not just Chinese businesses that manage to retain cash; memories of deprived childhoods have led members of the older generation to hold on to most of what they've earned. When they're not hoarding cash, they're using it to purchase everything from cars and houses to yachts and foreign luxury goods. Paper money was invented by seventh-century Chinese merchants. The Chinese government—the first to print paper money—consequently has no choice but to print more of it. China now accounts for about 40 percent of all global currency paper output. Printing bills in larger denominations is the logical answer, but the government, concerned that doing so would fuel inflation and facilitate easier payments to corrupt officials, refuses this straightforward solution.

CHAPTER FOURTEEN

China has become an economic world leader in a remarkably short period of time, but the reliability of its national accounts remains a matter of debate.

Institutional culpability is an issue with which the Chinese will be forced to contend in order to rebalance their economy from one driven by investment to one based on domestic demand. Petitioning the powerful—a practice in China for centuries—continues to substitute for legal process, and the Chinese judicial system almost always bends toward the interests of the state. Without laws of the land, business contracts between Chinese and Westerners are not binding, nor are there legal remedies to correct that frustrating injustice.

Released from accountability, or what Westerners believe to be the moral obligations of playing fair, the Chinese are not always of the mind that they need to pay Westerners what is owed, particularly when it comes to services. It's been my unfortunate—but by no means unusual—experience in China that when an inequity is revealed, it produces silence but not shame. Sometimes, though—when and where you least expect it—a business agreement falls effortlessly into place alongside its fair and forthcoming compensation.

That was the case with me and a Cantonese businessman.

Walking through the lobby of the St. Regis Beijing after a breakfast meeting, I passed the Chinese wife of a Western business associate. She introduced me to the man with whom she was chatting. He was extremely small and painfully shy and spoke no English. I offered two or three polite words and wished them a pleasant day. A few hours later, the woman phoned to explain that the man was a friend of the family and wished to extend an invitation to us both to come to Guang-zhou, where he was based when not in Beijing.

"Well, that's very generous of him," I told her. "But I'm scheduled for a working session with my book publisher here in Beijing at the end of the week."

"No, I mean this afternoon. He's inviting us to go this afternoon," she said.

"What kind of business is he in?" I asked.

"I told him about your background," she answered, deflect-ing my question.

"Where would we stay?" I asked.

"At his resort," she told me. "He owns a resort."

Two months before, I might have thought the proposition disturbingly odd. But living among the Chinese for that same period of time had enabled me to acknowledge that, yes, it was odd but, no, it was not necessarily disturbing. I flew to Guang-zhou that afternoon.

When we landed, the other passengers were kept in their seats while we were ushered to the front of the plane. The hatch opened, and there, directly in front of us, stood several mem-bers of what I assumed was the local police. They escorted us to a car parked on the tarmac to take us someplace. Where I could not say.

It was at this point I decided to press for more information.

"What would you like to know?" asked the woman who, just a few hours before, had convinced me to come.

"What is the name of our host?" was where I thought I should start.

She told me to refer to our host simply as Chairman. There was no "the" in front of Chairman, just Chairman. That a preceding article wasn't called on gave Chairman its celebrity-like ring.

Chinese capitalism consists of three interwoven categories:

state-owned capitalism, international capitalism, and private capitalism. The last of these blurs the boundary between reason and something else entirely. Chairman made his fortune in real estate, not an unfamiliar path to riches in China.

Because the Communist Party apparatus includes provincial-level governments, the provincial leaders have regionalized authority over large municipalities. And because those leaders' advancement in the party is based on their region's growth, it is not difficult to puzzle out why top local government officials are making the kind of decisions that will facilitate urban expansion.

Nor is it any wonder that many Chinese living in the country wish to move to the city. Urban residents receive state-allocated jobs and access to an array of social services currently denied to those living in the country. Given the inflated housing prices, it's a financial stretch for most Chinese to own their own homes. Complicating matters further is the contentious issue of the *hukou,* which has blocked those in rural areas from receiving the same social services as do city dwellers.

At the 2013 Third Plenum—a gathering of party leaders to set economic policy—there was an agreement in principle to strengthen land rights and shore up China's social safety net. But at the time I met Chairman, people seeking to move from the province in which they were registered—where they were born—needed governmental approval.

Chairman managed to put all of these challenges to work on his behalf. The scale of his real estate holdings—and his corresponding level of wealth—was extreme, even for China.

Guangzhou is a trading port and the capital of the province of Guangdong (historically known as Canton). Located on the Pearl River not far from Hong Kong, it is a key national transportation hub and the third-largest city in China, right behind Beijing and Shanghai.

Chairman owns a great deal of Guangzhou. How this impressive feat was accomplished touches on all aspects of the Chinese system, one in which politics and business work in a partnership driven by mutual self-interest.

Honoré de Balzac suggested that behind every great fortune in France was a crime. In China, it's not so much a crime but *guanxi*. Like the Chinese Thai, the Cantonese in southern China are known for their shrewd business sense. Chairman was somehow able to grant relocation permits to those agreeing to move into his apartment complexes in Guangzhou. The ever-increasing numbers of Guangzhou's new residents gave rise to his ownership of more and more residential buildings there, which in turn provided him the financial wherewithal to buy and build more and more of the city. It was a brilliant business model.

After amassing his billions, Chairman made arrangements for a huge temple gong to be loaded on a flatbed truck. The truck was driven to Conghua, where legend tells of *fenghuang,* the majestic Chinese Phoenix, which—so struck by the beauty of the mountains—stopped midway, in its journey across China's southern sky to rest there. Chairman instructed his security force to fan out and surround the Phoenix Mountains. The gong was struck, and as far as it could be heard, Chairman took possession of the land. On it he built an enormous resort complex designed to evoke an imperial hunting palace. He called it Imperial Springs.

My arrival at Imperial Springs unspooled with cinematic fluidity. Security guards saluted as our car drove through the arched entrance. That formality was repeated each time the car passed the numerous checkpoints, where yet more security guards wearing headphones announced me in advance to those waiting at my final destination. Lined up in a precise row in front of the enormous villa where I would stay were all five of my personal butlers, two of whom handed me a bouquet of flowers so large it had to be held by two more assistant butlers. My overnight bag was unpacked, the few clothes I'd brought were sprayed with rose water before being placed in a walk-in closet the size of most New York City apartments, and I was given a printed agenda of a tour that would stretch over the next two hours on acres of Crayola-green lawns and gardens that appeared computer enhanced.

What I saw would cheat anything in fiction.

Imperial Springs has a center equipped for corporate con-

ferences that includes a thousand-seat state-of-the-art audi-
torium with eight simultaneous translation booths and a
ballroom that can accommodate five hundred.

There is also a golf club with the confusing name of
International Summit. The twenty-seven-hole course features
remote-controlled electric golf carts that drive themselves. The
golf club resembles a larger version of the Gate of the Heavenly Peace in Tiananmen Square; its interior is borrowed from
Ralph Lauren.

Overlooking the resort is the presidential villa. With perfect feng shui, it backs onto the Phoenix Mountains and faces
the Liuxi River. The villa has a helicopter landing area, twenty-
eight bedrooms, twenty-four-hour butler service, a private chef
versed in international cuisine, and outdoor and indoor swimming pools. All of these amenities are scrupulously maintained
by a dedicated staff and await the president of a country, any
country. Alas, there have been no takers. But for those non-
presidential guests staying at Imperial Springs, there are, situated along the mountains, thirty-seven individual villas in the
traditional Chinese style.

The resort also boasts China's only all-suite hotel, a bar
that also functions as a giant humidor, and a spa with six treat-
ment rooms, each with its own radon-infused hot spring. There
is a private museum to house Chairman's art collection and a
separate living compound for the thousand people who work
at the resort.

Although Imperial Springs had been built two years before
my visit, Chairman could count the number of guests on one
hand. That face-losing fact was the troubling issue he wished
to discuss with me. But in China it is considered inexcusably
impolite to discuss business over the first meal, and so no business was mentioned during the elaborately staged dinner that
night. The meal began with a total of five rare Tibetan caterpillars being gently placed in my soup broth. Each cost a
hundred dollars, and the time-consuming presentation meant
I could not ignore the math. I was grateful that it took the
time it did to complete the ritual, for it ensured that—on the
off-chance they were still alive—the caterpillars would likely

drown before I was expected to show due appreciation by eating them one after the other.

It is a genetic understanding in China that you don't trust anyone but your family. And so it was Chairman's family I met the next day before an overture was made for me to become a consultant to his holding company, which controlled interests in a private bank, restaurants, hotels, and schools, in addition to Imperial Springs.

It wasn't until I flew back to Beijing with the woman who brought me that I heard the story behind International Summit, the golf club whose name makes no reference to golf. The Chinese are enthusiastic players of golf. It combines business with the obvious display of wealth: building golf courses in China requires a subsidized move of farmers off the land. For that reason, it is against the law to build a golf course on the mainland. Chairman built one nonetheless—three, as a matter of fact, and not one of them was referred to by what it was.

The caprices of the very rich in China are no different than those I've seen in any number of other countries, including my own. The morning I left Beijing for Guangzhou, *China Daily* ran an article on a certain tea that is grown by using panda droppings as fertilizer and costs $31,000 for five hundred grams. Chairman's wealth was made obvious not so much by his resort but by the fact he had three children. He had paid dearly for that privilege with something known as a "social compensation fee," a fine for the very rich that buys them dispensation from the one-child policy.

If—for whatever reason—Chairman had failed to reproduce, he would have been given the option to subcontract that task. For there are now agencies in China that cater to wealthy would-be parents by securing a birthing surrogate in America. When that child—born in the United States and thus a U.S. citizen—turns twenty-one, he can apply for green cards for his parents. In this way, some wealthy Chinese are ensuring their succession in China and, at the same time, are incubating backup plans to immigrate to the United States.

PART SIX

Children and Their Many Consequences

人之初, 性本善.

A child's life starts like one piece of white paper.
—*Chinese proverb*

CHAPTER FIFTEEN

Our Dongzhimen apartment looked out on one of the compound's several playgrounds, where ever-attentive nannies shadowed their single charges as if protecting perishables. Small, spry grandmothers used straw fans the size of elephant ears to cool down what would always be their only grandchild.

Like most apartment enclaves in Beijing, ours was enormous, and it was at its Olympic-size swimming pool one morning where I saw something plausible only in China.

Two women arrived with a little girl who looked no more than three years old. One of the women was the little girl's mother; the other, her nanny. While the nanny removed the little girl's clothes and replaced them with the bottom half of a bikini, the mother conferred with a young man dressed neatly in sports attire. He had a whistle around his neck and a small kickboard tucked under his arm. The little girl, familiar with the routine, held out her arms while the nanny made the necessary adjustments to her water wings. After a second check to make sure the water wings were secure, the nanny picked up the little girl and handed her to her mother, who handed her to the young man, who lowered her—now holding the kickboard—into the pool. He blew his whistle. The little girl kicked her way down the full length of the fifty-meter pool without stopping. As I watched her turn around and kick her way back, I thought to myself, *The rest of us have had it.*

The little girl kicking her way up and down the Olympic-size swimming pool was not the only example of supervised discipline among the children in our compound. As I left my apartment every morning for the market, I walked by a young boy being put through an impossible-looking regimen of table tennis. When I passed him on my way back several hours later, the poor boy—drenched in sweat—was still at it, relentlessly driving the ball across the net and returning it at lightning speed. I wondered if he was allowed the occasional pleasure of simply playing the game.

Physically precocious children appear in the crosshairs of their country's fixation on winning, and promising athletes are often plucked from their families at adolescence and sent to state-run sports academies. But the wider scope of pressure forced on the nation's children has been enabled by their parents' upward mobility. Chinese adolescents are swallowed whole by the schooling their parents can now afford.

Confucian principles dictate that the mastery of any subject is achieved only through long and exhaustive study. This fundamental tenet—that hard work and rote study trump creative discovery—echoes through Chinese history.

Each year, China's Ministry of Education is faced with the daunting task of educating over 250 million students; for the most part, it succeeds in that ambitious and admirable endeavor. According to the *CIA World Factbook,* China boasts a literacy rate of 95 percent. That the Chinese education system places an emphasis on high-pressure memorization and promotes standardization of knowledge over creative expression and independent thought is not without consequences. It has resulted in an intense work ethic, but it has also produced young people less capable of envisioning issues within a larger perspective.

China is undergoing an economic transformation ten times the speed of the West's Industrial Revolution, but for China to maintain its national growth, it must change its economic model from one based on manufacturing to one based on innovation. It is possible that China's educational system will prevent that metamorphosis.

Mei convinced me of this.

Mei and her parents lived on the same floor as we did in the Dongzhimen compound. Her mother was a doctor; her father, the editor of a business-to-business magazine specializing in aviation. Mei was twelve years old and attended a well-regarded middle school in another neighborhood. The school's reputation was based largely on the number of its students who were accepted into excellent high schools—high schools that had an impressive percentage of their graduates accepted into good universities.

Every weekday morning, Mei was up at six. She dressed, had breakfast with her mother, and was out the door by seven in order to make her first class at eight. Mei arrived at school fifteen to twenty minutes early so she wouldn't risk being late by one minute, for the school's strict attendance policy penalized tardiness. Mei's mother did her best to drive Mei to school, but sometimes Mei had to take public transportation; on those days, she started her commute even earlier.

Mei's class schedule depended on the day of the week and included the subjects of Chinese, mathematics, English, and history. There were also "electives," such as Chinese classical literature, which, though technically voluntary, were considered obligatory in light of the highly competitive nature of high school admissions.

In class, Mei sat quietly, listened intently, and took notes. She made herself known only to answer the occasional question from a teacher, which required naming a place or date. Regardless of the subject, the class structure was roughly the same: new material was presented, exercises were assigned to ensure that the material was properly processed, and weekly tests were given to confirm that the material was retained. Essays had a standardized format: students synthesized information they had been taught, drawing conclusions the teacher had already outlined for them. Standardization was rewarded. Diverging opinions resulted in lower grades, a risk not worth taking.

Mei finished school at five and immediately went to evening classes at a private cram school adjacent to her middle school. During her second shift of schooling, Mei reviewed the same material she'd studied in her day classes. She also learned various techniques designed to give her an edge on standardized tests. The evening classes finished at six-thirty, and Mei usually ate dinner on the same block as the cram school and with the same girlfriends who were attending the same school. Once home, Mei did several hours of homework, getting to bed no earlier than eleven. Every Saturday, a private tutor worked with Mei to improve her test-taking techniques. On Sunday, Mei did something she was not allowed to do for the six preceding days and nights: she put aside her schoolbooks.

Between 2005 and 2010, China's urban population increased by 43,500 every day, according the the Chinese National Bureau of Statistics. China's middle class will continue to grow at a staggering rate, and a correspondingly large number of students will flood the education system. Demand for higher education in China is outpacing supply, and two fundamental facts are creating a voraciously competitive student body: there are only so many hours in a day to study, and there will be more and more students applying for a finite number of openings at the prestigious universities. The year I knew Mei, seventy million high school seniors in China were vying for nine million university slots.

Given the incredibly competitive nature of the Chinese education system, any slip in Mei's schedule might have lowered her class rank, significantly lessening her chances at a successful future. Mei's father lacked the connections to guarantee his daughter's smooth transition into an elite high school, leaving Mei entirely dependent on her grades and test scores in order to stay on her upwardly mobile path.

Mei had a guitar, a gift from a relative, but she never learned to play it. It wasn't that Mei was uninterested in music. It had been deemed an "unuseful" activity by her parents. They believed that any activity not directly improving Mei's chances of getting into college was a liability.

Mei didn't know any boys. Her school separated the sexes in the classroom, and the teachers didn't encourage mixing on the playground. Mei's few girlfriends went to the same school, shared the same class schedule, and attended the same cram school. With the exception of occasional outings to a karaoke parlor to sing with these girls, Mei rarely saw them outside of school. Never would Mei consider confiding in them, for when the time came to apply to college, those same girls would be her competition.

Mei's life, as I came to know it, was typical for children in her family's socioeconomic bracket. Acceptance to a good university is believed to be crucial for a secure future in China—not so much for the quality of the education as for the status of attending the right school. The right school brings with it the likelihood of connections and the inevitability of a higher salary after graduation.

Tens of thousands of Meis are being shaped by China's educational system—a system that is not teaching the next generation how to think critically, a system that prevents creative spontaneity, a system unheeding of the cautionary warning of a Chinese proverb: "Do not confine your children to your own learning, for they were born in another time."

CHAPTER SIXTEEN

Western brands of academic elitism have colonized China.

The first to arrive was a satellite school for Harrow, followed by other franchises of Britain's best-known private schools. And newly wealthy Chinese are sending their children to American prep schools in the hopes of improving their chances of admission to brand-name Ivy League universities—a trend that has created the lucrative niche business of securing appropriate visas for Chinese parents to live in the States during the school year.

My son's deliberate reversal of this educational trajectory caused consternation among my Chinese friends. *What possible reason could there be to withhold an American education from your only child?* they would ask.

I won't deny that Gilliam's academic career had its own kind of burlesque staging. It was cast not by my academic aspirations for him, but by his unremitting personality. The dictionary features misleadingly similar definitions for the words "personality" and "character." In practice, they are different. Personality is a congregation of traits on the surface, while character has an interior foundation. There are subtleties to a personality, but character is fundamentally weak or strong and dictates virtually everything else. Even at its worst, an unappealing personality can never be as dangerous as a flawed character.

Where personality ends and character begins is a mystery

to me, but since personality is the totality of one's traits, I was struck that it appeared so early in Gilliam. When he learned to talk, what he said and how he said it spoke on behalf of his suspicion of anything that couldn't be proved. It was just a question of time before his unforgiving Cartesian logic would focus on his parents. This reason—more than any other—convinced W. and I to hand Gilliam over to the French when it came time for him to attend school.

The French system of education was created by Napoleon Bonaparte. It has changed little since. Homework is still done in fountain pen with blue ink, grades are publicly posted at the end of each week, and a mistake is worse than a mistake—it is a transgression. French students are on the same page of the same book on the same day, no matter where they are in the world.

Gilliam's list of school supplies for first grade warned me of what was to come. After searching through the *Larousse French-English, English-French Dictionary* for the better part of an hour, I managed to translate only two of thirty items: a large band to tie his books together and a small chalk slate for his class in mathematics.

The Lycée Français in Los Angeles is situated on a hill and housed in what was once Clara Bow's mansion. The school's old-style Hollywood backdrop adds to its intrinsic out-of-place aura. W. suggested we not tell Gilliam he would be attending a school where—with the exception of the English class—only French was spoken.

"The boy doesn't know what school is. He's never been, so how would he know what happens there?" argued W.

"It's lying by omission," I said.

"It's not lying. It's taking a position," insisted W.

"What position?" I asked.

"The one that gives us the upper hand for as long as possible," said W.

"He'll figure it out," I told W.

"Yes, but not right away," said W. "The important thing is to buy ourselves the time to get him to fluency; once he learns the language, the rest won't matter."

As soon as he got in the car at the end of his first day of school, Gilliam reported that, in case I hadn't understood, the school was run by French people. He pointed out that we were not French. He asked if we were planning to move to France. I said no. Then why was he in a French school?

Honesty was my only way out.

"You're there because it's important for you to learn another language," I said.

"Why?" asked Gilliam.

"Because the world is not just where we live," I told him. "Because the more languages you know, the more chances you have to know the world. The more you know the world, the more chances you have to make it a better place and the more chances you give yourself at an interesting life."

"Okay," agreed the boy. "I'll try."

For Gilliam to become fluent in a language neither of us spoke fluently, W. suggested we spend as much time as possible in French-speaking countries. I had limited opportunities away from work during Gilliam's school vacations, so my role in our travel *en famille* was telescoped into a few days at a time. The three of us would arrive at the designated location. I would settle them in, then turn around and go back to L.A.

Our first French language trip occurred the summer that Gilliam was between first and second grades. W. rented a house in southeast France from an old college friend. To say the house was rustic would have been generous. It was located in Combas, an absurdly small rural hamlet.

"I'm not sure I understand," I told W. "We have no directions and the town doesn't seem to be on a map. How will we find the house?"

"Apparently, Combas isn't far from Nîmes," said W. "We'll ask there."

Nîmes is located on the Via Domitia, a Roman road originally constructed to connect Italy to Spain. Its shield shows a crocodile chained to a palm tree. This is not as mysterious as it would seem when one learns that the city was settled by Roman legion veterans from Julius Caesar's Nile campaign who, having loyally served for no fewer than fifteen years, were granted plots of land to cultivate on the plain of Nîmes. The city had been one of the richest in Roman Gaul; its grand remains can be seen in the amphitheater in the middle of town, still used as a bullfighting arena. We rented a car and were pointed in the right direction for Combas.

Our rental turned out to be a seventeenth-century textile mill, one that had not been convincingly converted into a house. Instead of bathrooms, there were toilets behind closet doors, and the water pressure in the single makeshift shower was so anemic that it provided no more than a thick dribble. The first-floor hallway was as dark as a tunnel, and its ceiling wept with condensation that solidified into mineral stalactites. . . . The kitchen was an uneven, cave-like room that opened onto a garden with a wisteria-covered arbor, which harbored rabbits, neighborhood cats, and a loud magpie. None had the slightest qualm about joining us in the house when the back door was left open.

The village consisted of a cemetery and three narrow cobblestone lanes converging on a war statue marking its center. There was no grocery store, no bar, no bakery. Bread and eggs were sold in the mornings by a man from the closest town out of his van parked near the statue. So removed was Combas from the rest of the world that the townspeople would have been surprised if a family from Paris had arrived for the summer.

Gilliam came equipped with a universally recognized ice-breaker among children: a Game Boy. Within an hour of its being unpacked, everyone in the village under a certain age had congregated in our kitchen. That afternoon, I heard Gilliam's exuberant French swell and recede, depending on the level of gaming brinksmanship around the table. After the stone houses had absorbed the evening's cool air, the same gaggle of children appeared at our front door to invite Gilliam for a game of boules by moonlight.

Just at the time his whereabouts began to worry me, I heard him struggling with the thick wooden front door. He was holding a half-eaten baguette, his knee was scraped, he had a large clump of mud hanging from his hair, and his white polo shirt had acted as unprimed canvas for several large, oil-haloed stains of Nutella.

"What have you been up to?" I asked.

"Nothing," he said with a Cheshire cat expression of someone who had become a possessor of the town's secrets.

Four days in Combas was what I was given before business called me back to L.A. Gilliam and W. stayed on. By the end of their summer, when Gilliam talked in his sleep, it was in French. He returned to me in L.A. relaxed from country life, proficient in French, and newly devoted to Tintin comic books.

Georges Remi—a Belgian cartoonist better known as Hergé—was Tintin's French-speaking creator. He provided countless ports of call for Tintin, but no nationality or family. Unencumbered by the expectations of parents or the requirements of adulthood, Tintin is free to roam from one adventure to the next in Egypt, Peru, Scotland, Tibet, and even the moon. Accompanying him is a scrappy white terrier and a familiar roster of traveling companions. There is Captain Haddock, the bearded sailor who manages to function despite his precariously high levels of alcohol consumption. Several stories feature twin detectives almost identical: Thomson and Thompson. With the exception of Bianca Castafiore, an opera diva, few women join the adventures. In light of the single-sex odysseys, I was especially impressed that no matter how dangerous Tintin's situation—whether he's kidnapped, trapped, injured, under fire, lost, blackmailed, falsely accused of drug smuggling—his manners remain impeccable and his clean clothes beautifully pressed.

Gilliam's boyhood life was more regulated and less action packed than Tintin's. But it was almost as peripatetic, and the personalities in Tintin's world were all too recognizable in our own orbit of oddball friends.

Despite its small size, Belgium has managed to produce its fair share of cultural personalities. They—along with Gilliam's required fluency in French—were our reasons for the following summer in Belgium. Our chosen lodgings were in a converted castle on the outskirts of Bruges owned by a consortium of Belgian aristocrats who rented parts of it out. Rebuilt after the Second World War, it featured unused sitting and dining rooms on the ground floor and a warren of dark apartments above. To our relief, a French-speaking family moved into an apartment across the hall shortly after we did.

As was always the case, I had been given a limited period of time on foreign soil before the demands of my office returned me to L.A. While I was preparing to leave for the airport, Gilliam vanished in a game of hide-and-seek. When I asked one of the other boys to look for him in the garden, he called out, *"Guillaume! Guillaume! Viens ici, ta mère va partir!"*

My son emerged from the foliage; trotting not far behind were two other children from the newly arrived family. When I bent down to say my farewell, Gilliam kissed me in the Gallic manner: three times on alternate cheeks. He didn't return my "good-bye"; instead, he offered a French salutation that rolls easily from one good-bye to the next.

"À bientôt," said the boy.

PART SEVEN

Where the Chinese Dream Lives

有钱能使鬼推磨.

Money can buy a lot that is not even for sale.
—*Chinese proverb*

CHAPTER SEVENTEEN

Countless *à bientôts* were exchanged between me and my son over the course of his adolescence and young adulthood. One would come at the end of the summer in Beijing while I was writing my guide to Western business etiquette.

I'd been given three months to complete it, and that deadline required me to write two chapters weekly. Those two chapters were translated from English into Chinese by my publisher. The editor assigned to the project sent his margin notes in Chinese the following week. Gilliam's translation of the notes to English enabled me to adjust the two chapters according to the editor's requests and to return them—along with two newly written chapters—the next week.

Every day in China—with the exception of state-sanctioned holidays—is considered a potential workday, and so each morning at five, my paramilitary-like routine began at the kitchen table, where I wrote that week's two new chapters. A break came at nine, when I took the only form of exercise available, given the city's lung-destroying pollution: an hour of swimming laps in the compound's indoor pool. A late breakfast was followed by a much-cherished ritual made possible by Gilliam's technological cleverness. He was somehow able to download *The Daily Show with Jon Stewart* from his laptop and hook it up to the screen of our outdated and otherwise unused TV. After cleaning up, I continued to work on the new chapters while Gilliam translated the editor's comments on the previous two chapters. When Gilliam complained of hunger at midday, we struck out to explore an unknown section of the city.

Gigantic glass-and-steel buildings stood at attention on the inhospitably wide Second Ring Road circumnavigating our neighborhood. Those buildings appeared inaccessible and—on the whole—unfriendly. That impression hardened into factual dislike when I learned that the developers of a space-age-style building designed by the Pritzker Prize–winning architect Zaha Hadid had tried to ban the locals from participating in an annual craft beer festival on the grounds that the neighborhood's "homosexuals don't fit with the site's architecture." The stupefying declaration was such an achievement of distorted logic it required not only devoted prejudice but a blind eye.

My own architectural interests were located in what was left of the old city. And so our walks often led to the dwindling labyrinths of narrow streets, known as *hutongs,* formed by rows of *siheyuans,* courtyard residences that are the architectural opposites of the gladiatorial examples of China's determined modernity. With their beautifully carved roof beams and intricately painted pillars, *siheyuans,* some dating to the fifteenth century, were owned at one time by aristocrats, high-ranking officials, and wealthy merchants. Now they are multifamily dwellings connected to one another by interlacing lanes.

Westerners are prone to believe that China, at its political worst, is responsible for destroying individuality. But Chinese culture defines individuality by what precedes and follows a single life, and there has always been a collective nature to the Chinese people. "May it rain first on our public fields, and afterward, extend to our private ones" is a prayer found in the oldest Chinese scripture, *The Book of Odes.*

Deeply rooted in China's culture is the desire to conform to a unit. The people living in *hutongs* seemed to me especially happy. I was drawn to these Chekhovian hubs of activity, and it became our habit to eat lunch in front of the portable woks that lined the interconnected walkways.

There was an understood division of labor between Gilliam and me: I would commandeer one of the low makeshift tables and two rickety stools while Gilliam conferred with the mélange of vendors standing not much farther than an arm's length away but shouting nonetheless.

It was also the understanding between us that, as long as I remained ignorant of what we were eating, Gilliam had my preapproval in choosing our food. While I hold to the belief that in a foreign place one should try all manner of food, that did not oblige me to know what I was actually eating. Gilliam, on the other hand, was a genuine enthusiast. His unfettered approach to whatever foods happened to be on our plates came naturally, having taken hold long ago in L.A.

L.A. is a city accused of lacking a *there,* but, with a closer look, it reveals itself in hidden villages. When Gilliam was a little boy in L.A., his Sunday nights provided ritual delight for us both. I would send our globe into a slow spin with a gentle push. Eyes shut, Gilliam would bring his finger down. Eyes open, he would see where in the world his finger had landed. That place under his finger would be the country we explored for the week: the atlas was bedtime reading Monday through Thursday; Friday dinner was had in a restaurant serving that country's cuisine. During Gilliam's early childhood, we found our way to Bulgarian, Cambodian, Chinese, Indian, Israeli, Japanese, Korean, Polish, Portuguese, Russian, Samoan, Thai, Vietnamese, and Yugoslav cooking—all within driving distance.

I have eaten unbelievably exotic things in China. That cannot be said of the Chinese. They take very few culinary risks and, when traveling, are not particularly adventurous in sampling new foods.

The World Tourism Organization estimates that a hundred million Chinese tourists will travel abroad by 2020. Eventually, some of them will need to try foods they don't already know. I can sympathize, for just as the Chinese consider many foods eaten by others to be strange—cheese and butter being examples—I, too, have found myself confronted by local specialties that even a wicked boy intent on tormenting his little sister would not have the imagination to invent. I tried my best to remain open-minded when passing Chinese food stalls selling silkworms, grasshoppers, sea horses, and scorpions (stingers still intact), and with the exception of turtles, which have a sentimental place in my heart, I always ate what was placed in front of me by my hosts. Thus can I claim to have tasted snakehead soup, duck feet marinated in blood, pork lungs, and peacock and pig face (prepared by pouring hot tar in the head to remove the hair but not the skin).

For every action, there is a corresponding reaction. It is not difficult to imagine why, after partaking of unidentified Chinese dishes, I sometimes felt a frantic need to locate "the facilities"—a euphemism I'd been taught as a child—no matter how improbable their availability. Toilets in China require users to squat over a porcelain opening. Women are obviously expected to squat more often than men, and Western women can be put off by the calisthenic circumstances. I am no exception, and though I long ago learned to carry a purse-size packet of tissues while in foreign lands, I've often had to remind myself that everything is relative, including toilet standards. My most memorable facilities were forced upon me while my brother and I were crossing the open plains of Tanzania to track the gorillas in Rwanda. Our guide—brandishing a loaded rifle—stationed himself not far from the tree he designated.

"He makes it impossible for me," I complained to my brother.

"I don't see how," was his callously male retort.

"Of course you don't. How could you? You're a man. You can't imagine what it's like to balance yourself like a human tripod in front of a stranger . . . one who's wielding a weapon, no less."

"Get over it, Eden. You're literally a sitting target for the lions. You should be grateful someone with a gun is watching out."

Years later, I discovered a very different interpretation of "the facilities" when I traveled to Tokyo. Indeed, my first impression of Japan had to do with the elaborate—and some would say overly complicated—relationship the Japanese seem to have with their toilets. Drinking copious amounts of water during the ten-hour plane trip from New York had left me desperate by the time I arrived at the Hotel Okura. Grateful for the close proximity of the ladies' room to the lobby, I was confronted by a toilet that, instead of a handle, provided the choice of half a dozen buttons. With no obvious option for producing a flush, I was forced to try them all. None had to do with actually flushing the toilet. There was a button that shot an unexpected stream of warm water my way, and another offered music. There was even a button that mimicked the sound of a flush—the faux flushing to override the sound when, finally, thanks to the music, you were relaxed enough to perform. And if all else failed to cue your bodily need, the toilet was able to feign the sound of urinating, presumably to encourage a Pavlovian response—exactly the method the Chinese use with their babies. In most places in China, babies do not wear diapers but pants whose crotch seam is expediently split for when nature calls. *"Ssssss,"* a parent prompts, holding the baby in the direction of the wind and a safe distance from those passing by.

CHAPTER EIGHTEEN

China's government now protects *siheyuans* from being destroyed. But that doesn't mean they can't be moved, and I have met an extremely rich man who did precisely that. He paid a fortune to relocate several families living in a Beijing *siheyuan* and then spent another fortune moving the entire *siheyuan*—stone by ancient stone—to the roof of a five-star hotel. I speak here of a *siheyuan* built in the Ming dynasty and reincarnated as the penthouse of a luxury hotel so that its owner might enjoy room service.

Before the ebb tides of China's middle class began lapping onto the shores of communism, it was believed that love was built on a foundation of common political understanding and comradeship in work. Money was not a consideration in marriage because money was not the foundation of love.

No longer.

Today, a man in China who does not own a house is not considered very good marriage material, and pressures caused by the mainstream societal expectation of marriage and progeny have resulted in financial Darwinism among the army of young Chinese men coming of age.

The ostentatious display of home ownership in China is made more remarkable by the fact that most of the ground on which the Chinese stand—along with the buildings, residential and business alike—is government owned and leased for a curtailed period of fifty years.

China's government has claimed its legitimacy from the past ten years of growth, and grow the nation it must continue to do. The Communist Party's sweeping modernization plan is to move nine hundred million people—about 70 percent of the country's population—into newly constructed cities by 2025. This top-down mandate is meant to transform China's export-based economy into one whose growth is based on domestic demand for products, but acute problems with farmland rights and housing have deepened the class divide and bred public discontent.

The government hopes that by providing consumer credit it will propel consumer spending, which will result in a different kind of economic growth. But there are financial hazards to China's loosely regulated cash-borrowing options, and with no unified official procedure, registration of land-use rights falls under the jurisdiction of local authorities whose self-serving interpretation often invites corruption. Land can be expropriated for reasons of "public interest," the definition of which has been deliberately kept vague, which—deliberate or not—enables government officials and developers to dispossess farmers and pay them below-market prices for their land.

As a result of this rushed urbanization program, China's land-leasing winners are the developers who can flash enough money at real estate opportunities to make short-term sense. What is left in the wake of the country's binge growth is an eerily repetitive landscape seen even in the poorest parts of China, where luxury towers and monolithic office buildings stand empty and motorways end suddenly in a patch of gravel.

The theory behind China's urbanization—whereby newly created city dwellers will, of their own accord, create new business and break the cycle of those farming the land consuming only what they grow—has proved uneven in its implementation. Despite the promise of a permanent stream of revenue from the land they'll lose to developers, farmers are often unwilling to leave a life they know for one they don't. Pushback has come from bloggers born in the digital age and unafraid of writing about the forced evictions and the corruption in their communities. Pushing too hard brings a visit by the authorities for an informal interrogation, euphemistically known as *he cha*. The literal translation is "to drink tea," and it is one of many approaches to state censorship in China.

The Ministry of Industry and Information Technology, a parody unrivaled in name, is China's censor. When, in 2010, the Chinese civil rights activist Liu Xiaobo was awarded the Nobel Peace Prize, foreign news outlets covering the story were blocked. But blogging, already an integral part of Chinese urban culture, proved a formidable tool of instant communication.

The Chinese government is quick to learn, and has positioned itself in front of the inevitable consequences of its increasingly web-savvy citizens. Public security authorities follow citizen opinion with 8,583 official microblog sites on Weibo, China's Twitter-like website.

The party shapes its image by flooding popular web-based communities with pro-party opinions, by creating fake accounts in order to skew perceived opinion, and by paying people to post favorable sentiments about the government. The word *mao* has a denominational meaning of one-half a yuan. Rumor has it that each favorable post is rewarded with a *mao,* and so the Chinese slang for those paid to do so is *wumao.*

It is worth considering that Britain is estimated to have more security cameras recording its citizens—one for every eleven people—than any other country, including China. When I lived in London, I cared less and less about the cameras stationed in plain view. That might explain why, regardless of China's ubiquitous censorship, my daily life in Beijing didn't evoke the visceral feelings of oppression I've felt in Cuba and Russia, where cameras and microphones are installed out of sight. It might also be worth considering the idea of censorship from the Chinese perspective. Most Westerners forget that, over the past thirty years, five hundred million Chinese have been lifted out of poverty. They do not go hungry. They are employed. Their children are being educated. These are the unarguable results of China's one-party reform policies. Despite the fact that censorship is stitched into the fabric of their lives, the majority of Chinese people appear grateful for the advancements brought about by their government.

But things never stay the same. And the quest for personal fulfillment among a new generation of Chinese is threatening to create what might very well be impossible challenges, for the Chinese want what Westerners already have: things.

They also want to travel.

CHAPTER NINETEEN

Leisure travel is new to the Chinese.

In the past, arduous conditions prevented it for those adventurous enough to wander beyond the province of their birth. "The road to Sichuan is more difficult than that to heaven" was not much of an exaggeration. And if that warning weren't enough to keep the Chinese in one place, Confucius, who preached against journeys, believing they interfered with the importance of family, added his own guilt-inducing instruction: "While your parents are alive, it is better not to travel far away."

With the unstoppable rise of the Chinese middle class, tourism is expected to increase by double digits annually for years to come, but it wasn't until the late 1970s that the Chinese were permitted to travel even to Hong Kong to visit relatives. The country's economic momentum of the 1990s benefited its travel industry. Determined to encourage consumer spending, the government has purposely increased the number of mandatory public holidays in order to stimulate domestic tourism.

Gilliam and I decided to make a contribution to the Chinese economy by planning a trip to Nanjing, the capital of Jiangsu Province, in eastern China. It is a city with which Gilliam was familiar, having previously lived and worked there during an extended break between his freshman and sophomore years at his UK universiy.

I suggested we take the train.

"Are you sure?" asked Gilliam.

"What are you telling me?"

"That you might want to put some distance between yourself and your expectations. The last time I took the train to Nanjing, my seat partner was a rooster."

"Was it in a cage?" I asked.

"Yes . . ."

"Well, that's something," I said, determined to hold any second thoughts at bay.

"You're serious? You really want to take a train?" asked Gilliam a second and third time.

"The prices are unbelievably cheap," I told him. "We can afford to go first-class."

"First class in China is not the first class you probably have in mind," was the last of Gilliam's fair warnings.

"I grant you that, but I want to see what the train station looks like," I told him.

To commemorate the tenth anniversary of the founding of the People's Republic of China, the Communist Party constructed ten monumental buildings, the Beijing Railway Station being one. Experts from the Soviet Union were enlisted for their technical guidance, while two million Chinese construction workers completed the project in just over seven months. In 1959, Chairman Mao inaugurated the building by writing the calligraphic characters on the station sign as "The East Is Red" was played.

After being informed that the station's traffic surges to thousands of people during the day, I thought it best to take the overnight train.

"We still need to arrive well in advance," said Gilliam.

"I don't see why. I've already got our tickets," I pointed out.

"It's not like checking in at the airport with your executive platinum card," my son told me.

We arrived two hours before our train's ten o'clock departure and found the building's vast square crammed with travelers, most of whom were chain-smoking.

As a traveler of many foreign lands, I have come to believe

that one's mistrust should give way to fatalism when nothing else is clear. As soon as I realized we were at the mercy of fate, I succumbed to the train station's solid block of humanity. There was no space to sit—not even on our suitcases—and so we stood with hundreds of others, waiting to snake toward a location I couldn't see but assumed was the platform.

Gilliam is six foot five. With his imposing height and command of the language, he took the lead, and I held tightly to his shirttail.

By the time we made our way onto the platform, the crowd had thinned, but, strangely, those in our immediate area continued to crowd together. Twice I stepped away from a man standing too close before realizing that his cheek-by-jowl inclination was not the strategic positioning of a pickpocket, nor was it the precursor to a grope. It had to do with the absence of personal space in a country whose enormous population had long ago grown connective tissue.

Entering the first-class car, we shimmied sideways along a narrow hall. When finally we arrived at our compartment, I opened its door to a space so small that it was nearly impossible to close the door behind us once we'd stepped into it.

All twelve square feet of the cabin were covered in a layer of grime. The rancid smell of cigarette smoke permeated the bunk bed, which barely accommodated my full length and was half a foot shy of Gilliam's. As the train pulled away from the station, Gilliam and I sat side by side in dazed silence on the lower bunk, staring blankly at a dirty wall two feet in front of us.

I reached in my purse for the herbal sleep remedy purchased two months before from the *yao popo,* the medicine woman, in Dongzhimen to combat my jet lag when I first arrived in China. Sleep had come on its own that week. The tablets were left in my purse.

"What's that?" asked Gilliam as I unwrapped a compressed pellet of herbs from its rice paper.

"I either force sleep or throw myself off the train," I said.

"Be careful," suggested Gilliam, swinging himself onto the

upper berth. "Chinese herbs can be narcotic—and with you, cold medicine is a gateway drug."

I have a freakishly low resistance to pills and alcohol. Two aspirins have been known to put me in a slurred state. But this was different. After all, these were only dried herbs.

"I'm not worried," I told Gilliam before swallowing the bitter-tasting tablet. "The Chinese have used medicinals for centuries."

"But you don't speak Chinese. How did you manage to tell the *yao popo* what you wanted?" asked Gilliam. "Mother . . . ?"

Gilliam looked down to discover that I'd slumped into a comatose sleep. So quickly and completely had the herbs taken effect that my feet were still on the floor.

Gilliam breached male-female etiquette as he frantically sifted through the contents of my purse until he found a pocket mirror, which he shoved under my nose to make sure I was still breathing.

I woke the next morning with absolutely no recollection of the night before.

"You've got to get a grip on the language," Gilliam said in a severe tone.

"Please, no lectures," I told him. "I'm not feeling myself."

"I mean it. Don't go anywhere near the herbs again until you learn at least some Chinese."

"You're right. I'll try to learn more of the language," I promised. "Meanwhile, where are we exactly?" I asked.

Had I posed the same question in Chinese, it would have been as existential as it was practical, for Chinese verbs have no tense, and Chinese adjectives offer no degree of comparison.

Unlike my son, I have a problem learning other languages. Despite my periodic immersion in French, I have beaten all records in how long it has taken me to speak enough of it so that, while in France, I am able to make myself understood by small children and extremely slow-witted adults. Despite this linguistic humiliation, I can rightfully claim a well-informed impression about languages in general, and it seems to me that verbs are their cultural fulcrums.

Turkish verbs include a tense that distinguishes rumor from truth: a clever resource that enforces accountability. The canny French move in the opposite direction with verbs that are convoluted qualifiers. Sturdily independent, action-oriented Americans insist on forceful verbs, which the English subordinate after paving the way with countless niceties. I have been asked to pass the salt at an English table with an inquiry previewed by an apology: "I beg your pardon, but is the salt quite available?"

Verbs in China are unhampered by tense, which enables words to take an invisible leap from one topic, one person, one time to the next. Spoken Mandarin is replete with homophones. Its four tones, as well as the content of what one is saying, act to eliminate ambiguities.

Not for me.

To be fair, how was I expected to grasp the content of sentences that hang in the air attached to nothing at all? Even when I paid close attention, it was impossible to distinguish the four tonal differences. The slightest slip suddenly moved the meaning of a word in an unexpected direction. My mistakes became legendary. One was showcased at the conclusion of a business meeting in Shanghai when I thought I had requested a cab to take me back to the hotel but instead had unintentionally offered my sexual services. Although embarrassed by my declaration, none in the room looked displeased with its possibilities.

CHAPTER TWENTY

Nanjing is on the southern bank of the Yangtze River.

The city's name translates to "southern capital," since it was there that China's first Ming emperor established his capital. The West knows it for the Nanking Massacre, the systematic slaughter of an estimated 300,000 men, women, and children by Japanese troops during the Sino-Japanese War in 1937.

Roughly 170 Chinese cities have more than one million residents, exceeding the population of many countries. Only four of those cities—Beijing, Shanghai, Guangzhou, and Shenzhen—are considered first tier in terms of size and per capita gross domestic product. Nanjing's designation as a second-tier city strikes me as counterintuitive, for it bustles with commercial activity from all five of the so-called pillar industries: electronics, automobile production, petrochemical, iron and steel, and power.

Bicycles and tuk-tuks skirt the edge of Nanjing's constant flow of honking cars and trucks, cables crisscross its alleyways and streets like musical bars crowded on sheet music, and it is impossible to escape the noise from the city's never-ending construction.

Having spent the summer three years prior at the university in Nanjing to improve his Chinese, Gilliam made the decision to postpone the second year at his British university in order to work for a Nanjing businessman by the name of Han Ling.

Mr. Han's personal wealth counted in the millions, rather than the billions of Chairman. But his fortune, like Chairman's, came from real estate.

Serendipitous circumstances brought Gilliam and Mr. Han together. Gilliam was to tutor Mr. Han's son. Upon learning that Gilliam spoke French, Mr. Han hired him instead to work at his luxury jewelry company to resolve a predicament. It happened that Mr. Han had retained the consulting services of a very expensive French designer in Paris who spoke not a word of Chinese. Inconveniently, no one in Mr. Han's company spoke French. Gilliam spoke both languages. A tutor to Mr. Han's son one day and the director of international relations the next, Gilliam—at the age of nineteen—oversaw fifty-four employees.

The large number of employees in Mr. Han's company had to do with his background as a farmer, and his background as a farmer had to do with China's shifting policies of rural-land ownership.

In his relentless drive toward communism, Mao appropriated privately owned land from what he called China's "country landlords." That land became communal property, and the peasants working it were assigned collective ownership. Two decades later, Deng Xiaoping granted private ownership of land parcels to individual workers within the collectives.

The party's policies toward farmland ownership continued to change until they came full circle. Over the course of Mr. Han's life, he had worked the land as a child, owned it as a young man, and—in his middle age—sold it to developers. During the recent years of China's real estate boom, each one of Mr. Han's land deals led to another, more profitable one, and he became very rich—richer than the pre–Cultural Revolution landowners from whom the land was originally appropriated.

Had it not been for China's modernization program, Mr. Han's plan to launch a luxury retail brand would not have taken hold. Thanks to the party's stated intention to shift China toward a more consumer-oriented economy, the start-up costs for Mr. Han's company were covered by government subsidies. But the local official had a proviso: Mr. Han must employ the older men who had worked the farmland he'd sold to developers.

Unable to retrain the men who once worked his land, and intent on finding a way to ensure the continuation of government subsidies for his company—subsidies that would aid in the production of luxury goods for China's upper-middle class—Mr. Han added a room to his vast office compound where the older men spent their workdays smoking, playing cards, chatting with each other, and watching a large flat-screen TV.

More amazing than the jerry-rigged government subsidies for Mr. Han's company was its invented provenance. Extensive tax records were created to establish the history of a nonexistent aristocratic French family, one which had designed jewelry for European kings before fleeing France during the French Revolution and settling in Shanghai. How, generations later, the family came upon Mr. Han—a farmer who made good in a province thousands of miles away—is not explained. It need not be. For Mr. Han could produce the family's official crest, also fabricated. Flamboyantly false documents had been validated the moment the ink dried, and like much of contemporary China, Mr. Han's company had been successfully transformed from its novelization to nonfiction.

The convivial Mr. Han invited us to dinner our first night in Nanjing.

Gilliam—who would be staying with friends—dropped me off at a hotel I booked online, selected for its Western bathrooms. The hotel's website had made it look modern. It was anything but.

No matter, I thought. It would do for my two-night stay.

After unpacking, I decided on a bath. But there was no bathtub, despite the one pictured on the website.

No matter, I thought as I reached around the shower curtain and ran the hot water. Feeling the urge to make water of my own, I sat on the toilet. For a woman, sitting on a toilet is a mundane act done without thought any number of times during the course of a day. For me, this time was different.

There was the sound of crashing porcelain. Inexplicably,

I found myself sprawled on the floor. Staggering to my feet, I realized that the entire toilet had fallen over.

How could that possibly be? you might ask.

The answer is simple: the toilet was not a functioning toilet but a stage prop.

I shut the shower off and marched downstairs to the front desk. Lacking the words forced me to pantomime my discontent, but it is virtually impossible to mimic a toilet falling over. So I took the manager to my room and showed him the toilet—still on its side—and made myself understood: I wanted to be moved to another room, one with a toilet that was actually attached to the floor.

"Mr. Han asked that we meet him in his office first," said Gilliam when he came to the hotel to retrieve me. "He wants to give you a tour. Just nod and go along with everything he says."

"Is there a reason you're prepping me?" I asked.

"You'll see for yourself," was Gilliam's cryptic reply.

China's land supports a population six times as large as it was two centuries ago, and in some areas horticultural techniques have progressed little. Hoeing, transplanting, reaping, threshing, and digging ditches require backbreaking work. Years of physical labor had made Mr. Han look a great deal older than he was. His face was a topographical map of hollows, folds, and crevices. It was fairly obvious that no part of his personal wealth had been spent on a dentist or a tailor. Several of his teeth were missing, and his shirt was stained. The hacking cough plaguing him was a symptom of emphysema, which—if his nicotine-stained fingers were any indication—he appeared to be treating with cigarettes.

Mr. Han was a garrulous man whom I liked right away, and we exchanged mutually incomprehensible pleasantries.

"It is English soap for your wife," I explained as he sniffed the box I presented to him.

I gave him my second gift.

"The Cuban cigar is for you," I said. "Both gifts are special."

While Chinese politeness often assumes the shape of a gift, it doesn't prevent the question of how much the gift cost its bearer.

"Are they expensive?" asked Mr. Han.

"Yes, very expensive," I told him.

My claim was exaggerated for the sake of pleasing Mr. Han, who looked extremely pleased.

He began the tour of his office compound by proudly pointing to the large marble bust in the lobby. It was of the seventeenth-century French founder of the company.

Well, actually, no. It was a bust of Beethoven.

My face was quick to express confusion; just as quickly, Gilliam pulled me aside. "Don't ask any questions," he whispered as we were escorted to Mr. Han's private office.

He gestured for us to come to the other side of his desk, where his safe was located. It looked like something seen in old black-and-white movies. Carefully shielding the combination as he rotated the enormous ball-bearing lock, he struggled to pry open the heavy door, creating just enough space to reach in and remove what he explained was a very old document. Only it was new.

It diagrammed the entirely fabricated genealogy of an ancient French family. Another document I was shown pictured the family crest, which appeared to include the state flag of Hawaii.

"If you go to the trouble of falsifying your company's history, it should at least look historically accurate," I murmured to Gilliam as we followed Mr. Han to a restaurant on the second floor of the building next door, which he also owned.

We stepped into a private dining room flanked by giant cement foo dogs, and before we took our places at the table, the gruffly likable Mr. Han offered the first of what would be many toasts that evening by holding up his glass and saying, *"Ganbei."*

As is the practice in China, our host knocked back his glass of wine like a shot of tequila. He waited for me to follow suit, whereupon Gilliam took pains to explain that I had a medical condition and would, well, die if that kind of drinking was expected of me.

With its inky red color and a smell that reminded me of old leather bindings, I knew, even before tasting the wine poured to the very top of my glass, that it would be special. Rather than swigging it down, I did something that is perceived in China to be a social rejection of the host: I sipped. That first sip was warm reassurance that absolutely nothing could possibly go wrong as long as I took my time getting to the next.

Mr. Han—fearing I was dissatisfied with the wine because I was so slow drinking it—showed me the label on the bottle: Château Lafite Rothschild. All I could think of was that the price of that single bottle of wine—emptied during the first ten minutes of dinner that night—must have cost several times Mr. Han's total annual income years before.

The custom of toasting dates back to the Middle Ages, when people were not above poisoning their enemies' wine. To prove that the wine the host was serving at his table was not tainted, he would pour a small amount in his glass and that of his guest, and they would drink together, at the same time, in a display of mutual trust.

Chinese wines are made from any number of ingredients, including bamboo leaves, cassia flowers, and ginseng. All share a base of grain liquor. But China is also the world's biggest importer of Bordeaux wines, and it is soaking up top vintages. Wine consumption has doubled twice in the past five years, but *baijiu* remains the most popular liquor and is served liberally at dinners. So it was *baijiu*—between 80 and 120 proof and with its smell and taste of paint thinner—that was poured immediately after Mr. Han's obligatory display of Château Lafite Rothschild.

In China, toasts are not limited to the meal's beginning and ending. Instead, they are scattered generously throughout and announced with the word *ganbei,* which means "empty the glass." Half a glass of wine sipped slowly during the course of the entire meal is known to move me to something as close to louche as possible, so you can see where even just one *ganbei* might lead.

As treacherous as it can be for the guest, partaking in the inebriated merriment at a Chinese table is a sign of goodwill; denying that pleasure to the host brings a possible loss of face.

At banquets, it is not uncommon for the more savvy Western businessmen, aware of their own limitations, to be accompanied by a drinking stand-in. On one's own, it is best to employ false excuses based on health issues, for if you do not make a plausible excuse known before the first toast, you're in it for the long haul.

What fails to happen can matter as much as what happens, and declining anything from one's host in China—even with a seemingly legitimate excuse—throws a gloom over the shared celebration. As a guest of Mr. Han that evening, I moved out of my comfort zone to keep him happy. It takes only a few sips of alcohol to make the familiar seem strange to me, and the strange familiar. I began the evening with a straight-backed propriety, but sipping my way through the meal reduced me to a disheveled heap. When Mr. Han raised his glass to offer our final toast with the noxious *baijiu,* I slumped forward onto a plate in front of me of slices of dragon fruit and pineapple. Gilliam helped return me to an upright position for the sake of the toast. Black seeds from the dragon fruit stuck to my face.

Though my son was endlessly amused, having never seen me in such an undignified state, I was the only one at the table appalled by my condition. Rather than a sign of degradation, my inebriation was viewed as a welcomed show to Mr. Han that the elaborate dinner he hosted had been a great success. Staggering out of the restaurant—with no wish that anyone, including Gilliam, accompany me in my semiconscious haze—I insisted I could make it back to the hotel on my own.

Mercifully, the cool night air restored a degree of sobriety, and I reclaimed enough cognitive thought to decide to include a lesson on wine protocol in my book.

A splitting headache was waiting for me the next morning, but I managed to write the lesson on the practices of Western drinking. Its introductory sentence was banging against my brain as I wrote it.

→ *LESSON 16*

Most important, make sure you know your own limits in drinking alcohol. At the dining table, the bottle of wine should be placed in front of the host. If there are more than six guests, another bottle of wine should be stationed at the other end of the table.

If you are the host, it is nice—but not necessary—to offer your guests their choice of red or white, no matter what kind of meal you are serving. Wineglasses should be filled, from the right, half to two-thirds full. When pouring and refilling, it is best to hold the bottle around the label to prevent slippage and to twist the bottle slightly, which will disallow drops from falling from the neck of the bottle onto the tablecloth. If you are the guest, don't reach across the table for the wine. Wait for it to be offered. It is the prerogative of the host to offer the first toast. If it is apparent a toast is not forthcoming, a guest can propose the first toast (before people start eating) as a way of thanking the host for bringing everyone together and the hostess for her generous hospitality.

After I had composed this lesson on wine protocol, it occurred to me that there was another, separate issue that required equal consideration. Though unable to recall a great deal of the previous evening, I had a vivid recollection of the various noises made at the table, which convinced me to amend the lesson I had already written on table manners. Advice on the inadvisability of making noises—at and away from the dining table—required face-saving aplomb. I was able to provide some degree of it by drawing from my family experiences.

When W. and I were wed on the Amazon River by the captain of a Peruvian supply boat, the ceremony was followed by a feast of monkey meat. It was little wonder the legality of our marriage certificate didn't manage to make it across the border and we had no choice but to repeat the wedding in the States.

The week before, a distraught W. made a call to my office to inform me that he wanted to tell me something. He suggested discussing it over dinner that night.

I phoned Candida immediately. "What can it possibly be?" I asked her.

"He's already married," guessed Candida.

"That's ridiculous," I said. "He couldn't have hidden a wife—not for a year."

As the words crossed my lips, I remembered W.'s admiration of the man in the Amazon with two wives. When, that night, I met W. at the restaurant, the knot in my stomach had taken the place of an appetite.

W. and I sat facing each other across a table, and hovering directly above was a forbiddingly empty caption balloon. W. ate his dinner; I rearranged mine on my plate. W. lingered over dessert; I sipped tea. By the time W.'s espresso arrived, I couldn't stand waiting any longer.

"What was it you wanted to tell me?" I asked with an expression that projected mortification in advance.

"This is so embarrassing," was his ominous preamble. "If I tell you, you won't bolt, will you?"

Solidified fear lodged in my throat. "Of course not," I managed to say. It wasn't an entirely truthful answer.

"The thing is," he said in a voice that rose barely above a whisper, "I make a sound."

I was sure I'd misheard.

"I beg your pardon?"

"I make a sound," he repeated.

By no means did my confusion disappear, but overwhelming gratitude took over.

W. was relieved as well. "I feel better now that you know," he said.

"I'm glad you told me, darling, but we've been together for almost a year, and I think I've heard all the sounds in your repertoire."

"Not this one. I make it when I draw. You're not around when I draw."

As a cartoonist, W. worked from home. What he had said

was true: I left for my office in the early morning, before he sat down to draw, and I didn't return home until after he had put his drawings away for the evening. W. explained that he suppressed the noise during the weekends.

"What kind of noise is it?" I asked him.

"I can't tell you," he said. "But I gather it's loud. . . . I mean I've been told it's loud."

"How loud?"

"The couple who lives below us thinks I've set up a machine shop," said the man for whom I would forsake all others.

The noise made a point of introducing itself the day we would be joined in legal matrimony. The wedding was held on W.'s family ranch in Northern California. That morning—as I walked across the courtyard toward the cottage where W. was drawing—I heard what I assumed was the sound of farm equipment, but each step brought me closer to the realization that W. was powering the noise.

I stood outside the door long enough to decide not to open it. Instead, I went to the main house to have breakfast with my future mother-in-law. "How long has he made the noise?" I asked. "Since he was a little boy," she explained, as though it were the most natural thing in the world. "But I think it's better if you referred to it as a 'sound,'" she suggested. "It's a far more attractive word than 'noise,' wouldn't you agree?"

The Collinsworths were arriving later that morning. Each member of my family would display a uniquely disturbing brand of eccentricity; one in particular had required a three-day pass from a mental institution to make the trip. It seemed to me that I was in no position to ask questions I wasn't willing to answer myself.

"Of course, you're right," I told the woman W. loved best. "It's a sound, not a noise."

Despite my mother-in-law's distinction between making a noise and making a sound, it is equally likely that both—heard by those other than the Chinese—will result in varying degrees of embarrassment for Westerners. This I made clear in my amendment to the lesson on table manners.

CHAPTER TWENTY-ONE

I couldn't bring myself to visit the Nanjing Massacre Memorial Hall, which exhibits skeletons stacked in piles and old photographs of corpses lining the streets. Affirmation of life for me was to be found in a Muslim-style tomb containing the headgear of a fourteenth-century eunuch, buried at sea, whose expeditionary journeys from Nanjing reached as far as Southeast Asia, India, the Middle East, and East Africa.

Zheng He had been a mariner, an explorer, a diplomat, and the fleet commander of naval expeditions during the Ming dynasty. Years before my visit to Nanjing, I heard some part of his incredible story from a Chinese colleague in Shanghai. For fear of putting my colleague on the spot, I withheld questions, the first of which would have been the most obvious: Given Zheng He's dashing flair and unquestioned bravery, who would have deliberately truncated the physical evidence of his manhood—and why?

Answers were found in Nanjing.

Zheng He was captured as a child by the Ming army in Yunnan Province. He was castrated and placed in servitude to the emperor, whose son, Zhu Di, was Zheng's age. As a young man, Zheng accompanied Zhu Di on military campaigns against hostile Mongol tribes on the northern frontier, and thereby earned both Zhu Di's trust and respect.

With time, Zhu Di's armies would also occupy Nanjing.

When Zhu Di became emperor, he ordered his court in Nanjing to construct a vast armada of nearly two thousand trading vessels and warships and named Zheng He its commander in chief.

Zheng He returned from travels to Brunei, Thailand, India, the Horn of Africa, and Arabia with the exotic novelties of ostriches, zebras, and giraffes; and his fabled exploits were recorded by Western writers, who changed his name to Sinbad the Sailor.

After exhausting my way around all that had been memorialized of Zheng He in Nanjing, I did what I do in a city I do not know: I headed for the market. Regardless of where in the world they happen to be, open-air markets are always a lively congregation of everything local; the one in Nanjing was no exception.

I am not as tall as my son, but my height is still considered extreme in most parts of China, and people stare at me as though studying a creature capable of feeding from the topmost leaves on trees. I wandered the market in no particular direction but word traveled quickly—or so it seemed—for it was not too long before locals congregated in a semicircle, nodding among themselves as if agreeing on my oddity. After a short period of intense staring, some asked to take my picture, while others encouraged me in the direction of various food stalls. Trying my best to be agreeable, but unwilling to purchase skewers of squid and octopus, I sought safety in the market's grain stalls.

Grain has remained a dietary mainstay in China since Mao declared it so with the Great Leap Forward, a hideously misnamed campaign wherein thirty million people starved to death in an eight-year period. That human disaster was the result of the failed attempt at a nationwide communal agricultural production dictated by Mao's blind insistence that crop output would soar by appropriating private land for the purpose of forming farming communes, much like the one to which Mr. Han's parents were inducted.

Convinced that large reserves of grain would be the nation's security, Mao turned as much of the land as possible over to rice, wheat, and millet. Wild birds, considered poachers of grain, were ordered killed, and to make room for more cropland, hillsides were deforested, fruit trees were cut down, and ponds were filled in. Destruction of grasslands caused the soil erosion that is one of the many reasons for China's current urban pollution.

Mao's manic belief in grain was matched only by his obsession with the pig, an animal that nourishes itself with what it can scavenge and produces a nonstop supply of fertilizer for the crops. So prevalent is pork in China that the Chinese use their word for meat, *rou,* to mean pork unless otherwise specified.

The Chinese believe that eating specific animal parts contributes to human health. They are convinced, for example, that consuming fish eyes maintains ocular health. More ethereal properties are attributed to certain animals and are ascribed literal representations.

For the Chinese, the turtle is a symbol of wisdom, endurance, and long life, and it is thought that by eating turtles, one is granted those same benefits. It came as no surprise to me that turtles were sold in the Nanjing market. Indeed, I have seen turtles sold in Chinatown markets throughout the world.

It is possible that turtles, with a lineage extending back at least 230 million years, preceded dinosaurs. Their physical appearance has changed remarkably little since the original model. Because their hearts don't require a regular beat—and can be turned off and on at will—turtles have managed the enviable feat of slowing the aging process. I was especially pleased to learn that female turtles don't reach sexual maturity until their forties or fifties. Since turtles' shells are, in effect, the bones of the rib cage turned inside out, turtles cannot crawl out of them. They are deliberate-moving and very friendly looking creatures that can grow quite large—large enough to take up the entire width of a bathtub. I know this for a fact.

"HE'S IN THE BATHTUB," was six-year-old Gilliam's greeting when I returned home from the office one night.

At the time, we were living in L.A., and there were only two "he's" under our roof. One was standing in front of me, and the other took showers.

Aware of my husband's improvisational approach to parenthood and reminding myself that they had been left to their own devices the entire day—a school holiday—I realized as Gilliam took my hand to lead me to the bathroom that anything was possible.

Sitting in enough water to be reassured he was not entirely out of his element was a turtle so large that, had it not been alive in our bathroom, it could have been on taxidermic display at any number of natural history museums.

He stretched his stringy neck to its longest possible reach and moved his wizened face slowly from side to side. With his unblinking, upwardly tilted gaze, he must have seen that I was even more confused than he was. The only question that came from my open mouth would repeat itself throughout my son's early childhood:

"Where's your father?"

"Papa has gone to the store for dinner," said Gilliam. "Isn't he beautiful?"

"Yes . . . and what a surprise he is," was all I had a chance to say before I heard the garage door open and W. come in through the kitchen.

"Welcome home, my dear. I assume you've been introduced to the new member of our household."

"We've met. . . ."

"He's a beauty, isn't he?"

"Where in God's name did he come from?"

"He was meant to be lunch. Luckily for him, I happened to ask if the turtle soup was fresh," said W., uncorking a bottle of wine.

From this information, I assumed they had gone to L.A.'s Chinatown.

"Wonderful little restaurant," reported W. "No menu . . . two or three selections, . . . and when I asked about the turtle soup, the owner suggested that we see for ourselves. Gilly took one look at the turtles stacked in a wooden barrel and insisted we save one of them."

Elvira, the young nanny who lived with us during the week, listened politely to that evening's one-topic conversation. Refraining from expressing her opinion, she sat in quiet dignity, no doubt asking herself whether our benign eccentricities had taken a dangerous turn.

"He'll be a great addition to the koi pond," suggested W., referring to ours in the gardened courtyard behind the house.

"What will we feed him?" I asked.

"From the look of him, I'd say anything that happens to cross his path," said W, prompting me to inquire if anyone had seen our cat recently.

"Strawberries," suggested Gilliam. "He'll eat strawberries."

"It's not likely the turtle would enjoy strawberries, sweetheart," I said.

"You're wrong," Gilliam insisted. "Remember the one in the book? He loved strawberries."

"I don't remember that book," I had to admit.

It was only when Gilliam began to describe the story's characters that I realized he was referring to Gerald Durrell's account of his childhood in Corfu.

"Honey, that was a fairly small tortoise. This is a turtle— one that's apparently been on a regime of steroids."

"We need to start somewhere," Gilliam said.

"The boy has a point," suggested W.

"You do realize how odd all of this is, don't you?" I asked my husband.

"I think it's perfectly reasonable," insisted W.

I was sure reason would have disagreed, but I got into the car after dinner and drove to a grocery in Beverly Hills that stayed open late so that I could buy strawberries for a shockingly large turtle rescued by my son that afternoon from becoming soup stock in L.A.'s Chinatown.

There are few universal truths to which I can personally attest: one is that turtles go wild for strawberries. Certainly the turtle in our bathtub did that night, as did each of the ten turtles rescued from Chinatowns in the various other cities in which we lived during that period. A single lucky turtle was bought each year and released into whatever nature could be found in the city we happened to be living in that particular year. It was an annual rite known as the Turtle Release.

THERE WAS NO window of opportunity for the Turtle Release in Nanjing. Gilliam was with his friends for the day, and we were returning to Beijing that night. Making our departure fraught was a problem checking out of the hotel.

I had taken advantage of the modern convenience of the hotel safe and had stored my passport there. When the time came to retrieve it, the safe would not open. It required two hours and a crew of five to blast through the adjoining wall and into the safe. The deafening explosion left our ears ringing. My passport was returned to me still smoldering from gunpowder burns.

PART EIGHT

Getting from One Place to the Other

要前方路, 请问过来人.

If you want to know about the road ahead,
ask someone who has come back.

—*Chinese proverb*

CHAPTER TWENTY-TWO

Obtaining a passport in China has only recently become routine.

In 1994, the government allowed travelers access to non-Asian countries in a "planned, organized, and controlled manner." Since more and more Chinese travel abroad as part of organized tours, my editor requested I write a separate chapter on the logistics of longer journeys.

Why and how one takes a journey is inextricably linked to one's circumstances and age. Taken when I was very young and on my own, my first trip entailed enough planning to slip away from an attentive grown-up charged with my care. I must have considered the possibility of a long journey because I brought a loaf of bread. The milkman forced my journey to its premature conclusion when—spotting me walking purposely down the road—he returned me to my keeper.

Only now do I wonder what prompted me, at the age of five, to forfeit my childhood familiarity of place for the unpredictability of the unfamiliar. There was nothing in my life from which to run away, nor had there been a confrontation that morning that might have provoked me to punish the offending adult by leveraging worry over my disappearance. I can't say why I set off for a discovery, but it was urged on by a curiosity about what was being offered beyond the driveway, and like any journey, it required me to put my trust in Providence.

Writing travel tips for the Chinese fifty years later, I suggested that unexpected things can happen during a trip. My advice began with what to do before leaving on one. I was especially alert to the matter of passports and visas, so much so that I asked the editor to highlight the passage "Be sure that your passport is in order and that you have the proper visa to enter the country to which you are traveling." I had a personal reason for providing this advice.

IT TAKES REMARKABLY little to convince me to visit a place I've not yet been. A four-line passage written by Kipling was reason enough for a trip to Burma, a country now known as Myanmar.

Then, a golden mystery upheaved itself on the horizon—a beautiful winking wonder that blazed in the sun, of a shape that was neither Muslim dome nor Hindu temple-spire.

Built before Lord Buddha died around 483 B.C., the Shwedagon Pagoda is a 326-foot gold-gilded stupa on a hill overlooking the banks of a river in Burma. Kipling's description of it reverberated with such figurative and literary appeal that I suggested to W. we see it for ourselves.

At the time, Burma's constitution was suspended by a military junta.

"Let me ask you a question," said Jonathan after hearing my plans. "Do you have a death wish? Because I have to tell you, you're playing it out in a weirdly global way."

Jonathan is an investigative journalist so inclined toward suspicion that his desk area is referred to by colleagues as the grassy knoll. It is best to be direct with him; anything less encourages more of his questions.

"The pagoda we want to see happens to be located in a country with a history of internal struggle," I told him.

"'Internal struggle'? 'Protracted warfare' comes closer to describing its history," he suggested.

It was difficult to argue his point; at the time I decided to make the trip with W., the closest Burma had come to any semblance of stability was during its golden age in the eleventh century. Its last royal dynastic era was spent invading—or being invaded by—neighboring countries, until the English put an end to the warring by doing it better. The British eventually acceded to Burma's demands for independence, but internal disputes and political divisions challenged a democratic process. Things went from bad to worse.

That's where I came in—or, more accurately, where I did not.

W. decided to spend more time in Burma than I could afford out of the office; he left a week before I was to arrive. Chaos ensued when, at the last moment, the Burmese Embassy in Washington embargoed my passport without approving a visa. Both were returned in a frayed manila envelope that looked as if it had made the trip to Asia in my stead.

A single word derailed my chances of Burma.

"Publisher" was what I had written where the application asked for my profession. "Cartoonist" was how W. filled in his blank space—an obscure word with a vague enough definition to pass. At the last possible moment, I was denied access to a country in which W. had already been welcomed and was now waiting for me to arrive. The absurdity of our situation was a legacy of Orwell, who'd worked as a colonial policeman in Burma and would later write about his experiences.

Today's telecommunications make the most remote location instantly available. Back then the only means of communication was a landline, and there was virtually no time left before our scheduled rendezvous in Burma. I frantically tried locating W. When, finally, I was able to speak to him, the crackling static left our phone conversations pockmarked with missing words. "Can you . . . in India?" I asked. "I've looked on the map, and Madras has the closest airport. . . . I'll . . . next Wednesday."

Anxieties were allayed once we were able to realign our coordinates, but after hanging up the phone, I felt physically drained and terribly alone. I tried to remember previous times I'd been purposely kept from where I wanted, or needed, to be. The closest I'd come to rejection on the grounds of an arbitrary rule was when I was turned away at the door to a private club in New York where the publishing company I was running was holding a sales conference. Unfortunately, no one on the company's all-male sales staff was alert to the fact that my gender was not welcome at the club.

Had I arrived at the door with a communicable disease, I might have been greeted with more hospitality. Furious personnel—put off by the need to deal with an unexpected and unpleasant situation—isolated me in a remote corner of the lobby while they consulted the management. Thirty minutes later, I was allowed to walk a few yards beyond the area in which I'd been sequestered and into the room where my colleagues had also been kept waiting.

Being turned away at the door of a private club in New York was inconvenient but not noteworthy. My reaction to being prevented from traveling to a country—one that, ironically, had allowed in my notoriously unedited husband—forced me to admit I was an egregious example of entitlement. For me, access had gone without saying. I assumed the right to come and go, and when that right was withheld, it left me stunned.

My rejected visa application included its own interpretative Rorschach marks: there were smudges from what must have been a leaky pen and splatters of what looked to be coffee stains. How many hands had my application passed through before the decision was made to deny me Burma? I examined my returned passport; its earmarked pages were evidence of unrestricted travels. Each stamp on each page had allowed me a country and countless memories. But it was my own port of passage that had granted something far more profound than the possible view of an ancient pagoda. No matter how remote my journeys, that passport had steadfastly returned me to my country—a country whose foreign policies oftentimes run amok, but a country nonetheless unafraid of the word that named my profession.

→ *LESSON 17*

If you are going someplace you have not been before—especially if that place is a foreign country—read about its history and culture beforehand. Plan ahead as much as possible; gather as much information as you can online or through travel agencies. Find out if the country has any national holidays that fall during your visit. Confirm your plane and hotel reservations well ahead of time and again a few days before your departure. Before you pack, check with your airline to see if there are any limits on the size and number of bags allowed. Learn at least a few words of the native language, starting with "hello," "yes," "no," "please," and "thank you." Don't be loud in your speech. Understand the currency used in the country you are visiting.

The Chinese government, stressing that travel companies are now responsible for creating a good image of Chinese traveling abroad, has issued new tourism laws. The results have fallen short.

My lesson on international travel included the topic of pedestrian behavior on city sidewalks, for I cannot say just how many times I have emerged from a metro stop or made my way down a busy street in a Chinese city and smacked into someone in front of me who has come to a dead stop to check something or speak to someone in the coursing flow of a forward-moving crowd.

Taxis were also a subject of review. My advice there was not to push your way in front of someone who is already waiting for a cab—although that is very much the routine in New York.

Western tipping was a necessary but difficult subject for me to cover. As long as I can remember, I have suffered tremors of self-doubt from this arbitrary custom and cannot explain why, other than to point to the divide between what is expected from men and women. Over the years, and out of necessity, I have become fairly comfortable around a tool kit, but I am hopelessly mired in confusion when it comes to how much—and exactly when—I should tip. A bifurcated upbringing is to blame. My father demanded self-sufficiency; my mother insisted I hold to a stiffly defined code of conduct. Encrypted into her very being was a control panel that specified what to do and—just as important—what not to do in order to remain ladylike. It was acceptable to paint one's toenails during summer months. It was unacceptable to reach for the serving dish on a table unless it was one-half the distance of an outstretched arm. A lady didn't carry her glass of wine from a restaurant bar to the table. Under no circumstance was she to handle the logistics of tipping.

Business travel forced me to recognize the importance of how to tip, but truth be told, I remain at a loss even today. Can tipping the night manager at a hotel be misconstrued as condescension? Does one tip the porter at a similar level as the doorman? More to the point, is tipping a bribe to acquire good service, or a reward?

Happily for me—other than in Hong Kong and Macau—there is no tipping in China. That is certainly the case in Japan, where, during my first trip, a waiter ran after me in the street to return the money I'd left on the table. In most European countries, waiters are fully compensated by salary. Their service charge is featured on a separate line above the bill's total. The gesture of a gratuity comes from rounding up the bill's total with loose change left on the table. That is also the case in Britain, where, in Tudor times, the outstretched palm originated.

Americans, however, continue to hold fast to the ineffectual practice of tipping—ineffectual because in most restaurants tips are pooled, which leaves the person being served no opportunity to reward the person who has given good service and prevents an expression of displeasure if the opposite occurs. The best I could do with my advice on tipping for Chinese traveling to the United States was to recommend 20 percent in both restaurants and cabs, unless one's physical well-being had been threatened by partaking in either.

CHAPTER TWENTY-THREE

Publication of my book was scheduled for six months after I set foot in Beijing.

Gilliam stood in as my assistant and translator for the critical first three months. When he returned to England in the fall, I was left on my own with dangerously little fluency in Chinese, a tight book deadline, and an offer from Chairman to work for him as a part-time consultant.

Acutely aware of my need to function at full tilt and reminded on a daily basis of my inability to speak Chinese, I thought I should consider Chairman's offer, primarily because his Beijing office was in the same building as the St. Regis Hotel and my contractual arrangement with his company would include a residential apartment in the hotel.

There was, of course, another, overriding reason to accept the assignment. Given what I'd already seen of Chairman and his empire, I'd be a fool to walk away from the dramaturgical possibilities of remaining in his orbit.

Chairman's unbridled success could have happened as it did only among the Chinese in China. Americans doing business in China are hobbled by the U.S. Foreign Corrupt Practices Act. It spells out the illegality of securing "any improved advantage" with an exchange of favors, which is the very definition of *guanxi*. In plain language, that which is considered common business practice in China is considered collusion in the West. The view that China will eventually adjust to the West's moral code is an unworldly one, for the two cultures are not built around the same block of values.

"If not your family and friends, who else would you trust in business?" was the sensible-sounding question posed by a Chinese colleague when we were discussing *guanxi*.

Whether East and West will someday be capable of conducting business in the same way, I do not know. But I am convinced that observation moves us nearer to what is not necessarily known, and by proposing that I work with him, Chairman was offering a closer look at—what was, for me— the extreme unknown.

THE ST. REGIS HOTEL sits comfortably within the diplomatic district, an area in central Beijing that is home to foreign embassies. I missed the local color of Dongzhimen, but moving my base of operations was a necessary concession. The hotel's computer server is located in Hong Kong rather than mainland China, which enabled a relatively problem-free Internet connection. Its office center provided what I took for granted outside of China: a fax machine and a photocopier. Just as important, the hotel doormen spoke English and so would be able to explain to the taxi drivers where I needed to go.

The view from my apartment was of a block-long hole in the ground. Within six months, it would become a twenty-floor commercial building. From my vantage above, the construction site took on the appearance of a frenetically productive anthill. Scores of men—living in trailers on the rim of the hole—worked in shifts, seven days a week, twenty-four hours a day; at night, they wore hard hats with spotlights.

In my costly apartment above the fray, I was not unlike a guest on a luxury cruise ship with little need to disembark. Having been relieved of the nitty-gritty logistics required during my previous three months in China, determined to take advantage of the English-speaking, full-service aspects of living in the hotel, and refusing to be thrown off course by the fact that I had no real expertise on the subject of a book I was contracted to write, I kept to the same Calvinistic routine I had in Dongzhimen. Several hours of early-morning writing would precede laps in the hotel swimming pool, followed by a breakfast in the hotel restaurant of *congee,* a watery rice porridge, during which I read my way through the English-language *China Daily.*

Given my media background, I was impressed by the state-sponsored *China Daily.* Launched in the 1980s, at the time I first came to China, the newspaper is a single-minded publication that first tells you what your prejudices should be and then confirms them with carefully crafted anecdotes. I admired the perseverance of the editors, forced to comment day after day without a single piece of substantiated information, but I was also grateful for the more accurate debriefs of events in China during my periodic lunches with Jaime.

Jaime FlorCruz is his own remarkable story. Born in the Philippines and a vocal activist as a college student, he was forced into exile when Marcos—having declared martial law—decided to round up his detractors. Jaime was on the list of those who were to be arrested, but as fortune would have it, he was touring China at that very time. Stranded in China, he worked at a state farm in the Hunan Province to make enough money to travel to Beijing. Fluent in Chinese by the time he arrived in the city, Jaime was able to complete a degree in Chinese history from Peking University, after which he embarked on a career as a broadcast journalist. At the time we first met, he was the Beijing bureau chief for CNN.

As I was droning the obvious about *China Daily* during one of our regular lunches, Jaime made a suggestion.

"Read between the lines," he told me. "You'll learn that way."

He was right. By reading with a skeptical filter, I was able to gain a better understanding of the party's domestic policies, its attitude toward countries considered allies, and—more fundamentally—its take on right and wrong. Especially revealing was the paper's coverage of the 2012 London Summer Olympics, specifically when it came to the Chinese badminton team. They had been disqualified for deliberately losing one in a series of games by taking advantage of a technicality. To ensure that they advanced to the next round, they threw a game against a competitive team in order to win the next game against another, less formidable one.

Simply put, they cheated.

But the Chinese did not see it that way. They did not see it that way at all.

Outcry came the next morning from *China Daily,* which insisted that exploiting a loophole was not wrong.

My Talmudic-like concentration on *China Daily* during breakfast was occasionally interrupted when the word "joint venture" could be heard from the next table, proposed by an animated American to a tomb-faced Chinese businessman sitting across from him.

Other than me, there were two regulars at the St. Regis breakfast room. One was an elderly Chinese man who spoke impeccable English and eventually introduced himself as a onetime interpreter to Deng Xiaoping. The other was a Buddhist monk in a saffron-colored robe.

Why a Buddhist monk was eating breakfast by himself at the St. Regis Hotel every morning was a mystery that prompted me to consider the larger issue of religion—or, more precisely, the lack thereof—in China. While religions in most Western nations are significant cultural currents, that is not so in China, where the only native religion is Taoism. I doubt whether Taoism would even be considered a religion in the strict evangelical sense of the word, since it is an amalgam of philosophical concepts. When Mao called on individuals to sacrifice for the greater good of the people, it was not to instill altruism in the Judeo-Christian sense, but to strengthen the Communist Party.

Religion more than any other area has enjoyed the liberation of the post-Mao period. But at the core of contemporary Chinese society is a commitment to life as it is, not as it theoretically should be. That functionality has been what has allowed the Chinese to survive devastation after devastation borne by the twentieth century: the fall of the last dynasty, the chaos of the warlords, two brutal and overlapping wars (the Japanese occupation and a civil war), the disaster of Mao's utopian idea of the Great Leap Forward, and the murderous horrors of the Cultural Revolution.

At one time or another in their lives, most of the old in China have lost members of their families, their homes, their livelihoods, and their friends. Against all odds, they have managed to survive, but not by embracing that which the West might call compassion. And when Westerners gravitate toward sanctimonious judgment, as they often do, it is good for them to be reminded of the failures for which they, too, were responsible—as I was during my childhood holidays.

My father's interests included the study of Mesoamerica, and so my grade school vacations were spent at archaeological sites touring the dusty vestiges of ancient civilizations. Aztec and Mayan—with their symbolic allusions to the deities, the precision of their astronomical calculations, and the complexity of their calendars—were two cultures on which our itineraries would invariably concentrate.

Contrary to reason, these advanced societies also had an unfathomable capacity to kill. Clashes between city-states were ceaseless, and wars of conquest seemed to be the norm, some lasting more than a century.

"The arc of all civilizations includes the inevitability of organized inhumanity," was my father's grim pronouncement. We were visiting a Zapotec site at the time. The guide had directed our attention to an image etched in the floor under a door in what was, in 500 B.C., a public building. It showed a prisoner of war whose heart had been cut out while he was still alive. The Zapotecs memorialized the torture and murder of their captives on thresholds, explained the guide, so that whoever entered the buildings would step on the carvings, thereby further humiliating the memory of the enemy.

The evolutionary-shaped fact is that it's hard to be good. But we humans, apparently not compassionate by nature, are clever enough to realize that acts of compassion can facilitate the necessities of living together. I cannot say whether or not religion fosters compassion. China has never accepted the

Western ideal of religion, but its old people—whose hearts have been stripped of illusion and whose souls carry indelible marks of unspeakable cruelties—seem to have forgiven their fellow humans for what they have done to them. What is compassion, if not that?

CHAPTER TWENTY-FOUR

Buddhism in China is an import from India.

Chinese folklore tells of a time, two thousand years ago, when two priests, carrying Buddhist scriptures from India, were transported on a pure white horse to China. No one would claim that folklore brings with it a rational construct. But for anyone who has seen India, it is not difficult to imagine a white horse transporting two priests.

My first trip to India was the unavoidable result of being rerouted from Burma, which had denied me entry. But when I was a young girl, an Indian cultural attaché of sorts arrived on my doorstep.

He came in a huge storage truck that pulled up in front of our house several months after my father returned from a business trip to Asia. Two burly men rang the doorbell and handed my father's secretary—who was deliberately stationed at our home that day—a voluminous file of paperwork before they opened the truck's back doors. Tied down with the kind of thick rope used on a loading dock was a wooden crate almost the size of the truck itself. Great effort was made to unload the crate, and once it was moved out of the truck and onto the ground, crowbars were needed to pull apart its thick slatted sides.

What gradually emerged was an enormous statue protected by gauze and bulbous Bubble Wrap and standing upright in its own gigantic straw nest. The straw was plucked away, the Bubble Wrap was methodically removed, and layers of gauze were unfurled. It felt like an eternity before the excavation was complete and the object finally emerged from its mammoth cocoon.

What riveted me in place was not distinctly male or female, but the very definition of erotic: simultaneously unsettling and alluring. Its scale added to the drama, but scale was only one of what seemed myriad elements of its power.

The statue that held me spellbound was Shiva, the cosmic dancer who symbolizes nature's cycle of evolution.

With beauty that transcends gender, Shiva is male in name only. He has four arms. In his farthest right hand, he holds a drum, symbolizing the rhythm of creation; the open palm of the other right hand grants freedom from fear. The inner left palm, pointing to the floor, is salvation from ignorance. In the farthest left hand is held fire, symbolizing destruction. The left leg is lifted limberly in dance; the right tramples Apasmara, an ugly dwarf representing ignorance.

The powerful memory that underwrote years of my childhood imaginings lost its potency when, as an adult, I was able to place it in context. With a culture whose language was originally expressed in two thousand poems, the cities in southern India—including Madras—are dominated by some thirty thousand sanctuaries dedicated to their gods and goddesses.

Temple towns in southern India are religious complexes of enormous proportions, surrounded by fortress walls and entered by pyramidal gateways called *gopuras*. The precincts housed within are concentrically laid out in multiple walled enclosures. W. and I spent the better part of an afternoon in a temple complex, determined to locate its womb chamber, called a *garbhagriha*. The last we'd seen of anyone was in the outwardly ringed temples. With nothing but blind luck as a guide, we navigated the maze of pavilions and managed to reach the inner sanctuaries.

"It's just a question of time before we come face to face with the Minotaur," I joked as we threaded our way down a series of passages. We turned right at what appeared to be a juncture, but there was no sanctuary around the corner. Instead, we were funneled into the middle of a vast, pillared hallway.

Nothing could have prepared us for what happened next.

Coming around the corner and lumbering gently toward us was an albino elephant. He belonged in a dream: white as milk and draped in silk banners, his face elaborately painted. A silent Buddhist priest walked several steps behind.

We stood aside, in an electrified trance, for the elephant to pass. He stopped and turned to face us. His marble-blue eyes studied me carefully. My own stare glazed over until I registered the sweet hay smell of his breath the moment he raised his trunk directly above us.

Fearing I was just about to be struck, I instinctively braced my arms over my face for protection.

There was no blow to the head, but a tap.

As casually as he had stopped to acknowledge us, the magical beast continued down the columned hallway before turning toward a connecting chamber.

"What just happened?" I asked in bewilderment.

"I think he's blessed you," W. whispered, equally nonplussed.

We watched until the elephant's moon-white haunches— swaying as if in sync with the rhythm of time—gradually vanished.

THAT CHAIRMAN WAS a Buddhist came as no surprise to me. The atmospheric level of his wealth would have moved anyone into a Zen-like state. But creating a multibillion-dollar empire and keeping it whole in a country of constantly shifting political alliances is another thing entirely. Though Chairman carried an Australian passport, he spared no effort and expense in cultivating party connections, which resulted in *guanxi* enough for him to be driven, often with a police escort, in a van displaying Chinese military plates.

Chairman spent a billion dollars to build his Imperial Springs. That did not cover the construction of a private museum on its grounds, designed in the shape of a Shang bronze vessel. Nor did it include the cost of the museum's acquisitions. So vast is Chairman's museum that my private tour, led by its curator, took an entire afternoon.

Not even the curator knew where the museum's contents had been acquired, let alone how they were obtained or at what cost. One of some twenty thousand relics in the museum is a jewel-encrusted portable temple said to contain the cremated partial remains of Buddha. It was a gift to China from King Asoka, who ruled the better part of the Indian subcontinent in 269 B.C.

A supreme irony within the endless array of them in China is that ancient Chinese artworks that during the Cultural Revolution would have singled out their owners as enemies of the state are now eagerly sought by Chinese collectors, and that Chinese collectors are very much admired in China. At the opening celebration for dignitaries, the deputy governor of Guangdong Province toasted Chairman, declaring that the museum—which would never be made available to the public—showed "the true love that a leader of overseas Chinese has for his own country."

In my capacity as Chairman's consultant, I made fortnightly trips to Guangzhou to confer on various strategic issues. My first proposal was to form a partnership between Chairman's museum and either the Metropolitan Museum of Art in New York or the British Museum in London.

What might have been an opportunity became instead a series of obstacles.

Had I thought it through in the Chinese sense of thinking it through, I would have realized that inviting Western experts to a private museum in Guangzhou built by a mysterious Chinese businessman might lead to questions concerning the authenticity of its contents. Certainly the curator of Chairman's museum knew where my proposal would lead, and he would have sooner chewed broken glass than admit the museum's collection was riddled with forgeries. Rather than dealing with the matter, he stopped communicating with me.

Given the repressed manner in which I was brought up, it is unlikely that I will ever give verbal vent to what I actually feel. But my face, I am told, automatically announces a dramatic spectrum of my moods.

"Like watching an overacted four-act play in two minutes," Candida once described my facial expressions. She also told me: "If looks could kill, you could put those who displease you six feet under the frozen earth."

Despite my disappointment with the uncommunicative museum curator who left me in the lurch, an expression of arctic discontent did not find its way onto my face. There would have been no point, because blame is not a productive concept in China. Chinese people seem constitutionally incapable of self-correction and brook no excuses when things have been obviously mishandled.

It is helpful for a Westerner involved in any transaction in China to know that the classical character for the Chinese word "black" includes a subcharacter for the word "white." It makes sense, then, that the Chinese believe there are many ways to be right and that they are completely comfortable in what Westerners call a gray area.

Unfortunately, the provenance of several pieces in Chairman's museum had a black-and-white answer to the question of their authenticity, and I knew that worse than reporting facts of the matter would be Chairman's inevitable loss of face once I named them out loud.

As I finished explaining what he must have already known but did not wish to be told, Chairman looked resolutely unmoved.

The complicated system of interpersonal relationships among the Chinese depends almost entirely upon face. Loss of face is the inescapable proof in the eyes of others that you've managed to do something undeniably foolish. When face is in jeopardy, the solution is not to offer meek contrition but to retain whatever face is left with a blank expression. My tendency toward frankness is almost involuntary, but this time I made a concerted effort to couch it in as much deference as the situation allowed. Not wishing to forfeit whatever face was salvageable, Chairman met my disappointing news with a bland appearance of businesslike normalcy.

Realizing that open and robust business debates in China are hampered by the dread of giving offense, I thought to include a lesson in my book on how to respectfully disagree. It was a risky enterprise, for to argue a point in China—no matter how politely—is seen as impertinent.

→ *LESSON 18*

Expressing a difference of opinion among business colleagues in the most constructive manner possible requires one thing: an outward show of respect toward the person or people with whom you disagree. Do not call into question a person's opinion on an issue in a group meeting; instead, resolve your disagreement one on one. Think through the issue beforehand, and state the area of agreement first. Remember the small courtesies, and introduce your opinion politely by saying, "That's an interesting point, but have you thought about it this way?" Communicate your opinion clearly, and allow the person to respond without interrupting. Listen to the other person's opinion, and keep an open mind. If there seems to be confusion on the point you have made, clarify that point; however, don't repeat the same point too often. If someone disagrees with you, it doesn't mean they don't understand what you are saying. End the conversation pleasantly.

Self-assertion is totally alien to every inborn idea of what is correct among Chinese people. The lesson I wrote on how to disagree was met with skepticism by my editor. He agreed to include it in the book with the understanding that a lesson on how to apologize would appear in the same chapter.

→ *LESSON 19*

When accepting an apology, offer a reassuring smile, respond positively, and move on. Statements like "I'm sure you didn't mean it" and "I know how you feel, so don't worry, but thank you for your apology" are just right.

An apology should be short and sincere. Most people simply want you to acknowledge that you are aware of the fact that you have shown disrespect. "I'm terribly sorry if there has been a misunderstanding" is one way of neutralizing the situation when you don't believe you have done anything wrong but the other person obviously thinks you have. "You're absolutely right, and I apologize" is a way of gracefully admitting you have been wrong. Regardless of how you make an apology, don't dwell on it; say it with meaning once and move on.

Unconvinced that an apology on its own would make up for the potential disaster of being direct, the editor requested that I also include a lesson on how to offer a compliment— presumably to offset with obsequiousness an apology that would fall short.

→ *LESSON 20*

You can pay a compliment on anything that attracts your attention: wonderful food, if someone is entertaining you; or a business achievement, if you are among colleagues in a work setting. Your aim is to make people feel good. Offering a compliment to anyone—regardless of where or in what circumstance or country—is always flattering and always welcome. You'll be surprised by the positive results.

Compliments should be short. Sincere praise should be expressed in a few words. There is a fine line between complimenting someone and being too flattering. If you go overboard, your sincerity will be called into question, so don't overdo it. One thoughtful compliment is enough.

PART NINE

The Politics of Censorship

要使人不知, 除非己莫为.

If you walk on snow, you cannot hide your footprints.
—*Chinese proverb*

CHAPTER TWENTY-FIVE

My solitary hours writing comportment lessons sequestered in a hotel apartment produced an intense appreciation for daily walks. One afternoon, I noticed light-colored corrugated tiles in the middle of sidewalks not far from the hotel. The tiles formed narrow and fractured pathways that ignored the trajectories of the sidewalks in which they were embedded. One led up to a tree and, rather than loop around, simply reappeared on the tree's other side. Another vanished altogether, like the unfinished motorways in the middle of China's countryside.

I asked the hotel manager the purpose for the disoriented tile paths.

"The paths are for the blind," he explained.

"But they lead straight into danger."

The manager laid out his defense.

"No, madam," said he.

I decided not to argue, but I took to heart what was left unsaid.

THE CORNEA IS the transparent outer lens of the eye. Providing most of the eye's optical power, it covers the iris, pupil, and anterior chamber, which contains the retina. There are five layers of cornea. The summer I was seventeen, a rogue virus ate through four of the five corneal layers of my eyes. It only took four days—one day for each layer—for most of my vision to disappear. Just like that.

I assume the Fates decided that eliminating the better part of my sight was not melodramatic enough, because they added debilitating pain. The virus attacked and destroyed my corneal nerve endings and, like nuclear waste, wantonly leveled everything in its path. Though one eye in particular was under attack, the other suffered the same searing sensation of being stabbed with an ice pick. "Sympathetic pain" was what it was called, but no one could provide an explanation. In fact, the very identity of the virus eluded the medical experts. When there was nothing more to destroy, the mysterious virus departed as quickly as it had arrived. In its wake: one eye, a chalky blue-white, was made opaque by scar tissue; the other, barely functioning, remained a defiant, angry blood-red.

"Donor material" is the euphemism for corneas from a recently deceased person who, beforehand, possessed both foresight and generosity. After placing my name on a list, I waited for someone to die and leave me his eyes. Because the donor material couldn't be refrigerated, I would be required to arrive at the hospital at a moment's notice. In an age before mobile phones, the wait held me hostage in a small Boston apartment from which there was no stepping out, even briefly.

The Chinese have always believed that music reaches the world of souls and spirits. When I lost my sight, music transported me to that invisible world. Isaac Albéniz led me on walks in the Spanish countryside. Percy Grainger invited me to stroll in English gardens. Aaron Copland serenaded me down the Grand Canyon. Gustav Holst swept me through the firmament. My imagination was put into service, and—not always, but sometimes—the difference between what I heard and what I imagined seeing was indistinguishable.

"The Fourth of July weekend is only a week away," was the pep talk from one of the well-meaning doctors who had signed onto my case. "There'll be plenty of traffic fatalities," he reassured me.

———

IF PROUST WAS right and the real voyage of discovery consists not in seeking new landscapes but in having new eyes, I am that literal interpretation. It was a fifty-year-old man—killed not in holiday traffic but by a brain tumor—who returned my vision. My eyes have now accumulated more than a century of sight on behalf of both genders, and I am fortunate to be able to see clearly that which lies ahead of me, including China's antithetical pathways for the blind.

THERE WERE OTHER, more lighthearted discoveries made in the immediate area of the St. Regis Hotel.

One was a neighborhood called Yabaolu. The name means "elegant treasure road" and had been beautified from the original Yaba Hutong, or "mute man's alley." Business signs there are in Russian written in Cyrillic. The ethnic enclave consists predominately of fur traders from Siberia, but there are also Poles and Ukrainians who owned pelt stalls on what is appropriately named Alien Street.

Directly across from Alien Street is the relative quiet of Ritan Park. One of four royal shrines, it was built in 1530 as a place of worship for the Ming and Qing imperial courts. Within its walls is an eleven-hundred-year-old cypress with twisting, upwardly pointing branches. Not far from the ancient tree, old women practice traditional dance and old men do tai chi in the mornings. Skulking around the periphery are feral cats.

In preparation for the 2008 Summer Olympics, Beijing's homeless were shipped away and the thousands of cats roaming the city were rounded up. Both the homeless and the cats returned, and though it is not accepted practice among the Chinese to feed the homeless, cats are another matter. In the late afternoons—before it becomes dark—legions of cats tentatively emerge from the city's nooks to be fed by the old people. Their increasing numbers in the park might explain the corresponding decrease in the number of squirrels, and the reason cameras come out whenever a lone squirrel is spotted.

Unlike the Chinese, I am not charmed by squirrels, the result of an unattractive encounter with one years ago in New York.

Admittedly, I made the mistake of feeding the squirrel when he first appeared on the windowsill of my brownstone apartment. A shelled walnut gave the squirrel an excellent reason to reappear the next morning. Summarily ignoring our cat on the other side of the glass, the squirrel stood on his hind legs in order to make eye contact with me. He waited expectantly for a repeat of the walnut. When it wasn't offered, he defecated on the sill. His effrontery disgusted me and appalled the cat.

On the third morning, the squirrel scratched furiously at the windowpane, and the darker implications began to sink in.

By the fourth morning—when I realized I was being prevented from cracking the window to let in fresh air—the squirrel lost all charm.

I opened the window and sprayed him in the face with glass cleaner. He staggered backward and fell off the sill.

Having survived my frontal attack, the squirrel launched a devastating one of his own. I came home from work to discover he'd dug up all three of my carefully cultivated window boxes. It was brazen destruction of personal property, and I was left with no choice but to call an exterminator.

"What will it take to get rid of him?" I asked.

"He has to be caught and moved," he said.

"Fine," I agreed. "But I don't want him killed. Once you've caught the squirrel, throw a sheet over the trap, walk it across the street, and let him out in Central Park."

"It's not that simple," said the exterminator. "Squirrels have incredible homing instincts. He'll need to be relocated on the other side of a body of water so he doesn't find his way back."

"Jesus, this sounds more complicated than the witness protection program. What about the other side of the Turtle Pond behind the zoo?"

"That's too close."

"How about the reservoir on Ninetieth Street?"

"That will work," said the exterminator. "I'll be at your apartment Monday morning."

"Is that the soonest you can come? I can't crack any of the windows. The damn thing will squeeze through."

"We don't work on weekends. Monday morning, I'll set the trap. You'll find him in it by the time you come home. Store it in your basement overnight and I'll pick it up Tuesday morning."

"Wait, do you mean I store the trap with the squirrel in it?"

"Yeah."

"Overnight?"

"Yeah."

"No, I'm not going to store the squirrel in the basement of a brownstone building. I'll meet you at the apartment at three o'clock on Monday. I promise, if food is involved, the squirrel will show up."

On the designated day, at the designated time, I left the office to watch someone charge me a small fortune to bait a squirrel cage with a tablespoon of peanut butter. The trap was placed on the window ledge. Not one minute later, the squirrel appeared. So nonchalant was he that when the trap door shut, he didn't bother looking up.

"Will you drive your car up in front of the building?" asked the exterminator as he lifted the trapped but unconcerned squirrel through the open window and into my apartment.

"I don't keep a car in the city," I said.

"Well, how am I supposed to get the squirrel to the reservoir?"

"Are you telling me that you took public transportation to get here?"

"That's right."

"You never said anything about a car. And I have to get back to the office for a four o'clock meeting. I'll put you in a cab."

"Lady, not even a New York cabdriver will pick me up when he sees what I'm carrying."

"Well, just what do you suggest we do?" I asked, restraining my temper.

"What about a car service?" he suggested.

Twenty minutes later, a town car arrived in front of my apartment to transport the squirrel, along with his real estate broker, to the Upper West Side of Manhattan.

The expense of my New York encounter with the squirrel did not endear me to the few that appeared in Ritan Park. But I do share the Chinese people's fondness for ducks. Tucked in one of the pathways behind the park was a makeshift storefront no larger than a phone booth belonging to an old man who fixed bags, belts, and shoes. I brought all of my leather items under the pretense of repair so that I could check the progress of an orphaned duckling that trailed behind the man's small dog—small because owning a not-small dog is technically illegal in China, though Chairman's family had two extremely large Labrador retrievers in snow white.

CHAPTER TWENTY-SIX

In the opposite direction of the leather man, his dog, and his duckling was the Silk Market. Its eponymous product is sold on the third floor and takes up only a very small part of the large market, which contains some seventeen hundred retail stalls filled to the brim with knockoffs of Western brands of clothing, makeup, suitcases, toys, ties, digital cameras, mobile phones, binoculars, and everything in between. China's stance on the issue of trademark infringement appears on an enormous red sign at the main entrance, which states—without the slightest trace of parody—that all goods in the market are guaranteed to be authentic and of good quality. Unprepared tourists are seen reduced to tears as they try to fend off aggressive salesgirls accosting them in the aisles. With no set prices, bargaining is a process of one-upmanship played out on calculators.

Less chaotic is Panjiayuan, Beijing's giant flea market. Known as the "dirt market" because it was exaggeratedly claimed that peasants would cart in objects they'd unearthed, it features every imaginable curio and antique, including snuff bottles, porcelain bowls, Tibetan beads, white jade, bronze wares, and paintings of landscapes on long rolls of silk and paper. My regular sojourns to Panjiayuan were in the company of Roger, a colleague since my days at Hearst. His Saturday visits to the market had stretched over twenty years.

Roger appeared to have stepped out of a Graham Greene novel. He wrote poetry, spoke several Asian languages, possessed a Homeric knowledge of Asia-related matters, had belonged to the Australian foreign service, and had at one point very likely been a spy. By the time we met, he held a senior post at Phoenix Satellite Television, a major TV station in China not owned or run by the state.

Adding to Roger's aura of mystery was his impressively large collection of Chinese erotica. That he was a gentleman provided us with the unspoken understanding that I would never see this collection. It also allowed me an unencumbered friendship not only with him but with his delightful wife and daughter.

Erotica in China can be traced to the first century. It featured an infinitely diverse range of sexual prospects performed in ambitiously acrobatic positions often by more than two people. Chinese erotica flourished in the tenth century, when it drew its influence from the courtesan culture of the imperial courts. At some point in the seventeenth century, China adopted an extreme prudishness and erotica was forbidden.

In the Confucian *Analects,* it reads, "The Master said, 'I have never met a man who loves ethics more than he does sex,'" which presupposes that the former precludes the latter. The Cultural Revolution renounced sexual impulses and demanded they be redirected to the political cause. Mao institutionalized the separation of the sexes, an instinct that still remains among young people in China. In general, sex has been relegated to the functional purpose of reproducing and—to a measured degree—reserved for physical gratification within marriage. Premarital sex is not considered an aspiration of women's liberation. However, I've seen sex shops in China, even though pornography is illegal there.

There is sex and there is love, and, in China, it seems the two are not well known to each other. Love poetry in classical Chinese literature never achieved the same sublime rank it did in Western literature. Even with their low-tide approach, romance poems were reinterpreted as moral allegories by Confucius. Centuries later, communism assigned the idea of love a devotional purpose, grounded in sociopolitical issues.

Roger's attitude toward his erotica collection was in keeping with China's tradition of discretion. I was never shown the artifacts he considered purchasing at Panjiayuan, and we sought common ground in the market's erotica-free zone of the bookstalls.

Points of interest beyond Beijing's various markets required me to learn the city's metro stops. One brought me to the Military Museum of the Chinese People's Revolution, a war museum, featuring row upon row of antiquated tanks, each with a sign: MADE IN CHINA. Cutting across Tiananmen Square afterward, I stopped to study an enormous obelisk that is the Monument to the People's Heroes. Not far from the monument was a conclave of young men lingering around something I was unable to make out. As a foreigner, I would impart validity to whatever it was that was being deliberately obscured by the crowd, and so those standing next to me urged those standing in front to give way so I might see.

In the center was a young man holding a long calligraphy brush. I watched as he dipped the brush in a sawed-off plastic Coke bottle filled with dirty water and wrote hurriedly on the pavement. The approach of an army officer scattered the crowd. I was left standing over words of dissent compressed into a few quick characters. Flung fearlessly on the pavement, they lasted the short time it took for them to be absorbed by the cement.

China has come by its reputation for censorship without apology. Logging on to any public server in mainland China—including those at the increasing number of Starbucks coffeehouses—requires your cell phone number. Newsstands do not carry English-language newspapers or magazines, and even publications sold at the airports are tampered with. I realized just how hands-on the censors are with their vetting process when I purchased *The Economist* at Guangzhou's airport and discovered pages missing. From the cover line, I assumed what had been ripped out was an article on China's Politburo, the nerve center of the government. When I returned the magazine to the vendor and asked for another copy, he told me that all of the magazines featured the same omission and that the pages were torn out on the loading dock before the magazines had been delivered. Visualizing the logistics of what that entailed was enough for me to realize the Ministry of Information's maniacal level of operational efficiency. Recently, it has required that some 307,000 Chinese reporters, editors, and broadcasters attend a mandatory two-day course on Marxism, presumably a prerequisite to keep their press passes.

Although privately and publicly held media companies exist in China, the Western ones are limited to a minority ownership, and those run by the state retain a significant market share. The State Administration of Radio, Film, and Television and the General Administration of Press and Publication set strict regulations on taboo subjects. Topics disallowed coverage in the media are not dissimilar to those banned from debate in universities.

Paper, printing, and dictionaries—all Chinese inventions—have been subordinated by the Internet and its wraparound influence. How long China's newly empowered citizens—most of whom have access to the web on handheld devices—will continue to cooperate with their one-party government, which operates on its own timetable and according to its own needs, is another question entirely.

In addition to my work with Chairman, I had a consulting arrangement with another Chinese businessman. In a grand gesture to impress the Chinese delegation he was traveling to London with, he purchased a British cable station during the course of their trip. Returning to Beijing a week later, the man had no idea what to do with the station. At his request, I met with a senior officer in China's State Council Information Office, a government agency that now includes the Internet Affairs Bureau. I was impressed with the young man in charge, but he gave me no way of knowing whom, exactly, he was representing: the government or my client.

Both, it turns out.

The State Council Information Office has been mandated

by the party to ensure that news from China is justly represented in Western markets. Impressive inroads have been made. *China Daily* began to appear in various foreign editions during the time I was writing *The Tao of Improving Your Likability*. Since then, its management has entered into co-ventures with cash-strapped non-Chinese media companies. Censored news from China is now distributed by Western newspapers, which are coproducing—and inserting in their pages—special sections of *China Daily*.

While China's narrow version of the news is widening its global distribution, Western hotels are the only local outlets selling the *Financial Times* and *The New York Times*. Those same hotels, along with diplomatic compounds, have access to the BBC, CNN, and Bloomberg News, but it is believed that CNN's broadcast agreement with China stipulates that the network's signal must first pass through a Chinese-controlled satellite. Blacked-out content comes in broad strokes: reports of unrest in Tibet, tainted food, and Chinese dissidents are three of the usual suspects. When warranted, China's censorship can drill down to specifics. During the state-run China Central Television's coverage of President Obama's first inaugural address, there was no audio when he spoke of how "earlier generations faced down fascism and communism."

In addition to censoring information, China manages its own news. Though that process lacks subtlety when dealing with political criticism, it is an effective means of covering natural disasters in China, of which there are many. Immediately after a horrific earthquake while I was there, all Western broadcast stations were blocked in Western hotels and compounds. For three days, I watched identical footage, appearing simultaneously on all channels, of the Chinese army rescuing devastated villagers. No broadcast advertising was allowed for those same three days, and print advertising was banned from showing people smiling.

CHAPTER TWENTY-SEVEN

China Central Television, CCTV, is the nation's largest network. The sequential launch of its various channels speaks for the nation's cultural agenda. CCTV-1, its general programming channel, was launched in 1958, followed by CCTV-2, its finance channel, in 1963. Six years later came the arts-focused CCTV-3. Launched in 1992, CCTV-4, the network's international channel, spawned CCTV channels for Europe and America. Subsequent channels were devoted to sports, the military and agriculture, and Chinese opera. The most recent channel—and a personal favorite—is the Chinese version of an entertainment channel. It airs soap operas and game shows.

One of China's more popular soap operas is a historical romance that tells the story of Zhenhuan, an imperial concubine during the Qing dynasty. Possessing unmatched beauty and fierce intelligence, Zhenhuan manages to rise above the other concubines—and even the empress—to become the emperor's favorite and the most powerful woman at court.

Women prevailing against the odds seems to offer universal appeal, for I have viewed variations on that theme on television screens wherever I've traveled, including the unlikely location of Santiago de Compostela.

The name of this city in Galicia in northwestern Spain means St. James in the Field of Stars, and it has a long history of drawing travelers from distant parts of the world. Legend has it that the bones of the Apostle James made their way to the Iberian Peninsula for burial and were eventually discovered by a Galician shepherd who was guided to the spot by a star. A church built over the relics was later replaced by the Cathedral of Santiago de Compostela, which became the destination of the medieval pilgrimage route known as the Way of St. James.

"How did the bones get to Spain in the first place?" asked Gilliam when he was a boy and I suggested a trip there.

It was a fair question. Before I could consider it, he was already on to the next.

"What proof is there that they're actually his bones? And I don't believe the part about the star. It's always used to move the plot ahead when they can't explain the story."

"It's a legend," I pointed out. "Legends require a leap of faith."

"Just how far of a leap?" he asked.

"Granted, this particular legend doesn't make a great deal of sense," I admitted. "But it's been a destination for pilgrims for a thousand years. Aren't you interested in seeing why?"

He didn't answer.

"Come on, Gilly, we'll have a good time there. It will be like *The Canterbury Tales*."

"Because that book was so much fun," he said snidely.

I realized I was losing control of the decision-making process.

"No more sarcasm. I found a very reasonable hotel. We're going."

The Hostal dos Reis Católicos in Santiago de Compostela, thought to be the oldest hotel in the world, is also considered one of the most beautiful. An e-mail alerted me to its off-season rates and, ten days later, we arrived at its massive baroque door.

The rate was wildly out of step with the beautifully appointed twin-bedded room and the level of luxury we enjoyed for three days. Breakfast featured an abundance of local produce. Afternoon tea was served in the grand sitting room, where we were offered the traditional sweet pancakes known as *filloas*. Dinners, none costing more than thirty dollars for the both of us, centered on local fishes and meats cooked in the Galician way.

Gilliam was too young then to be allowed to explore on his own. That level of independence would not be sanctioned for several more years. He and I were stuck with one another twenty-four hours a day, and we had entirely different approaches to exploring Santiago de Compostela. I read guidebooks, with the intention of getting us to what had already been identified as worthwhile during our limited days. Gilliam wanted to enjoy himself without the burden of an agenda.

"No more of the cathedral, no more churches, no more Museum of Tapestries," he grumbled at the end of our first day.

"All right," I muttered without thinking. I was propped up in one of the two canopied beds, reading. The boy flopped down on the other, with his feet facing me and his focus on the television. Switching from one channel to the next, he paused on a quiz show.

"Sweetheart, can you turn that down."

"You should watch this."

"It's too loud," I said. "Please turn down the volume."

"No, I really mean it, you need to see this."

I peered over my reading glasses. There, on the screen, was a young woman made older-looking by makeup. Bleached blond hair and a silver lamé dress cast her in an oddly metallic light. Her ample bosom was straining against the plunging neckline of her tight dress. Having lived in L.A., where plastic surgery is a local craft, it is relatively easy for me to recognize surgically enhanced breasts—they often are seen preceding their owners into a room. But what took this artificially voluptuous and inappropriately dressed young woman from vulgar to intriguing was the fact that she was seated on a sofa in front of an elegant Georgian silver tea service, casually chatting with a nicely dressed young man seated on the couch next to her. Both of them were facing the studio audience. She hadn't served the tea yet. She would soon. It was expected by the young man sitting next to her, by the audience, by Gilliam, and, now, by me.

There was something else about the woman and her situation, something that undercut the expected act of serving tea.

She was wearing snorkeling goggles, the lenses of which had been blackened out, making it impossible for her to see.

In openmouthed wonder, I asked my son a question I would have spoken out loud had I been the only one in the room.

"What is *that*?"

"They're gigantic breasts," he said, having no need for more sophisticated analysis.

The book I was reading dropped to the side. My eyes narrowed on details while my brain tried its best. As it stood, very little was clear except that what I was seeing was inconceivable.

Gilliam's fluency in French brought him close to a Spanish understanding of what she was poised to do. "The audience bets on whether she can pour the tea without spilling," he explained.

"She'll spill," I said.

"Who cares? It's funny," said the boy.

That it was. And so was the game show I would watch regularly during my residency at the St. Regis Hotel in Beijing. The program featured women wearing panda ears while competing to win a date with a man they must first serenade in a karaoke contest. It surprised me. Not the panda ears. Pandas are almost an obsession in China. Not the karaoke. Karaoke is wildly popular among Chinese youth. The girls' deliberately short skirts teasing to reveal what was underneath: that surprised me. Overt sexuality is frowned upon in China, so the young women on the game show seemed to be beaming out mixed signals.

If asked to identify the most likely qualifier for professional success—be it for a man or a woman, a manager or an employee—I would answer that it is respect. Inherent in the meaning of respect—whether granted by the person to whom you report or by the person who reports to you—is how it's been earned and how it's been kept. Gaining professional respect is more difficult for women than for men. Often that unfair fact is through no fault of their own. However, it can sometimes be the result of how women present themselves to men—reason enough for me to write a lesson on appropriate dress for women in the office.

→ *LESSON 21*

If in doubt about appropriate attire, remember that underdressing is always better than overdressing. A woman's dress or appearance should not detract from her ability to conduct business.

You need not have a great deal of money to dress well. If you keep your wardrobe simple, it's hard to go wrong. You will get the best use from (and look the best in) clothes that are simple and fit properly. Never buy anything for just one occasion.

> WOMEN'S FASHION MISTAKES IN THE OFFICE:
> · Clothing that is too tight, too short, or too revealing
> · Visible panty lines
> · Gaping blouses that show skin or underwear
> · Torn hems and exposed linings
> · Overly dressy or too-high heels
> · Too much jewelry or makeup

My lesson on women's attire in the workplace concluded with the wisdom of an old Chinese proverb: "Do not dress in clothes made of leaves when going to put out a fire."

The managerial obstacles I confronted in business did, indeed, require me to put out fires. In those cases, I made a point of wearing fire-retardant gear.

PART TEN

The Body of the Workplace

盛喜中勿許人物, 盛怒中勿答人書.

Don't promise something when you are full of joy;
don't answer letters when you are full of anger.

—*Chinese proverb*

CHAPTER TWENTY-EIGHT

Approaching my tenth year as a corporate officer at Hearst, I received an unexpected job offer from the most unlikely place: a global think tank whose remit of conflict resolution is focused on security issues.

Had conventional thinking been allowed to interfere, I might have addressed any number of points—the most obvious being that I had no experience in world politics. But there were other, less obvious factors to consider. Gilliam was becoming a young man, and my custodial role was diminishing. Since I had put aside enough for what would be four years of his college tuition, I had less need to earn a certain level of income. To a measurable degree, I could afford to leave money on the table in order to do something I hadn't considered, something that would force my abilities to work against habit and would take me to parts of the world to which I wouldn't otherwise be going. Nothing in my life insisted on where I needed to be, and so I accepted an offer too improbable to refuse and became the chief of staff of a global think tank.

With its beginnings during the Cold War, the institute operated behind the scenes on matters that included cyber-security and weapons of mass destruction. Sixteen languages were spoken among its fellows and staff in offices located in New York, Brussels, Moscow, and Washington, D.C. Home for me became Brussels, as well as New York.

My friends wondered if I had taken leave of my judgment.

Annie looked conflicted during my summary of a Russia–U.S. joint threat assessment on short-range missiles. An expert on Cuba who at one time interviewed Castro, Annie knew of such matters.

"I don't see you in this space," was her reaction.

Jonathan acknowledged my concern about Yemen's water crisis but told me he needed a second martini if I expected him to listen to more.

Candida was not so patient.

"I don't know what you're talking about," were the sharp words she used to cut me off when, during a phone conversation, I launched into the topic of Afghan narco-trafficking.

"Do you want me to explain?"

"No."

There was a moment of dead-end silence.

"Are you the only woman in this organization?" she asked.

Her question had no claim to what preceded it but called forth the initial impression I'd had of the institute's offices. Drably painted walls and a heartless arrangement of furniture hadn't volunteered the slightest suggestion of women on the premises.

When she realized I would not be answering the question, Candida offered sympathy.

"It must be tough for you to be surrounded with nothing but men," she said. "Have they made you cry yet?"

In its shape and consistency, the human brain is like two handfuls of a pinkish-gray flan-like substance. Composed of a hundred billion nerve cells, the brain is the most complex of all biological expressions. To a large degree, it makes you who you are. Assuming the brain is the director of how one thinks, I cannot help believing it also rules the configuration of female and male thought—heresy coming from a woman born in the generation that was the first to insist on freedom from gender bias in the workforce. Still, I believe that the fundamental fact that I am female governs the way I think—the mechanics of how I think. I believe it for two reasons: I've seen it in ways that can be measured over the span of my career, and I have read the warnings issued by the Beijing Municipal Public Security Bureau on its Weibo page about women who drive cars.

"Some women lack a sense of direction," is how it begins.

Fair enough. For years, I was operating under the misimpression that when I was driving uphill, I was going north.

"Often women can't decide which way to go when they drive," the warning specifies.

On that point, I beg to differ. Women know where they're supposed to go. Often, they cannot find the right way to get there. Unlike men, women ask for directions. Admittedly, traffic accidents can occur if directions are asked for while in motion.

"Women drivers are prone to panic after an accident," states the bureau.

Dissecting the issue with a mock-scientific approach, the bureau uses the example of a woman who—having lost her composure after running over a pedestrian—got out of her car without locking the car door behind her. As a result, her purse was stolen.

Here, I am guilty, for I would not take the time to lock my car door before checking on someone I'd just run over. And even though I'm known for my reserve, I am certain I would fall apart were I to kill someone.

It is worth admitting that my estrogen-driven level of composure has yet to be tested in the way that would satisfy the Beijing Municipal Public Security Bureau. But during many years of working with men in business, I've struggled mightily at times to maintain outward composure and inward resolve. Still, the bottom line is what usually mattered, and no one argued with my revenue-producing results. Corporations like Hearst measure and reward performance based on generated revenue and profit margin, while the think tank, a nonprofit institute, used a less accountable method of identifying progress. It also had a more liberal interpretation of professional behavior. When I arrived, I was startled by the operatic mood swings and the unchecked aggression with which some of the men bullied their way forward.

Pride prevented me from admitting it, but there were men

at the institute who did, in fact, make me cry. That display of managerial weakness was withheld until the end of the day, when I went home, drew a hot bath, and allowed myself to break down. It took several sobbing baths to identify the interlocking issues of my predicament.

After thinking it through, I decided to call out the troublemakers and make my intentions known to each of them. The bombastic man who talked over everyone in meetings was warned that if he continued, he would be excused from the room. Another who refused to operate within his department's budget was informed that any deficit would be deducted from his salary.

The most combative of the men—a veritable signpost for post-reason anger—would become offended at the slightest provocation and disappear to sulk. At one point, he went MIA, and we finally located him on a different continent in a hospital recovering from the flare-up of his spleen, damaged years before when he was pushed out of an airplane. How or why he was pushed out of an airplane was never revealed. Truth be told, I, too, would have done the same, given the chance.

After dealing with the institute's operational issues, I focused next on the staff's appearance. All of the men had advanced degrees and many of them were brilliant. That did nothing to increase the extremely low standards had by some when it came to comportment. They seemed not to have had the time or energy to shave successfully. One in particular felt no need to use deodorant, and the odorous outcome resided among the rest of us.

To address these intrusively personal matters, I employed the Chinese approach to saving face by using Western tools of etiquette. Waiting until the conclusion of a staff meeting one Friday afternoon, I pointed out—in choreographed order— that the weather had become warmer, that our dated offices lacked proper ventilation, and that we all needed to pay more attention to practices of hygiene. Reminding the staff of the diplomatic remit of the institute, I suggested that poor hygiene distracts from meaningful intention.

CHAPTER TWENTY-NINE

By its nature patriarchal, Chinese culture has always assigned value to the serene and harmonious qualities of women—qualities in conflict with the workplace, an environment that requires directness. But it is also true that the idea of authoritative voice has proved to be a difficult concept even for Western women in business, who are capable of going to the core of an issue but seem unable to express exactly what they want when they get there.

I am not sure if it is the universal nature of women to avoid directness for fear of being perceived as unfeminine, but I am certain that the life I've had in business has forced me to compartmentalize my feelings in order to move forward. Whether my gender impeded my career advancement was, for me, not the point. I was determined to find interesting ways to earn a living.

Like it or not, there is a pecking order within any group, and ascending the hierarchy—any hierarchy—requires conformity. Conform I did, but without becoming too enamored of convention. It seemed to me that convention served a purpose, but it also had a tendency to ignore the more intriguing opportunities.

On my first trip to Beijing years ago, I was ushered into cavernous government rooms and sat in oversize armchairs sipping green tea alongside ministers who were what remained of the Red Guard. They told me that "women hold up half the sky." The only other women in the rooms were serving us tea.

This was not the case when, several years later, I visited China's Communist cousin, Cuba. Annie—absorbed in writing a book about Fidel Castro—had told me Cuba was crumbling and I should go there before it reduced itself to rubble. After taking the precaution of removing my business cards from my wallet, I arrived in still-embargoed Havana to see it for myself.

Annie was right. Cuba was crumbling. It was also jailing its dissidents.

But one of the few encouraging signs of the country's progress seemed to be the constitution, which prohibits gender discrimination and enforces equal pay for women. Unlike women in China, Cuban women are elected often to serve as cabinet members and mayors. Women make up 62 percent of the country's college students and 61 percent of its attorneys. Oddly, these encouraging statistics have had a negative impact on the traditional idea of a family unit in Cuba.

Cuban women's financial independence has resulted in their newfound self-confidence, which in turn has brought about intolerance toward routine infidelity among Latin American men, and Cuba, a predominately Catholic country, has witnessed a dramatic increase in its divorce rate.

Though women account for 74 percent of China's workforce, young Chinese women are constrained by traditional societal views whose resounding message—spoken even on women's leadership panels at Chinese economic forums—is that they will succeed only when men do. While the Russian blueprint for socialism provided women in Cuba professional and economic advancement, that has not necessarily been the case for women in China, whose culture is rooted in Confucian principles based on a distinct male-female hierarchy. Those principles have suppressed a routine advancement of women to high-ranking positions within government and business—and they have also failed to keep China's divorce rate down.

Divorce in China has increased dramatically for reasons

having to do with regulations aimed at curbing property speculation. A couple selling a second home has to pay a hefty capital gains tax on the profit; there is no tax, however, for a single
seller. Since Chinese officials are not required to ask the reason
for a divorce, couples divorce in order to avoid the tax but still
stay together.

I am not being falsely modest when I say that at no point
did I think that my own experiences or their linear extrapola-
tions were germane to women in China. Nor did I believe that
the advice I gave in my book would make a profound difference in how Chinese women think of themselves, given their
Confucian-based beliefs. So I deliberately stayed away from
esoteric issues and provided the kind of tactical advice I would
offer any woman. I emphasized that the ability to disagree con-
structively and negotiate effectively is imperative. I explained
that men and women communicate differently.

One of the first students from mainland China to attend
Columbia Journalism School and armed with China's equivalent of a doctorate, Li Qin is a young woman who is acutely
self-aware and decidedly unmarried. When we were introduced, she was in the process of launching a Beijing company
that offered a full range of cross-media marketing platforms to
Chinese municipal governments and businesses. Ten years on,
her clients include CCTV and the Ministry of Culture, and I
have joined her company's board as a nonexecutive director.

Confucian beliefs dictate that a good leader makes for a
good people, that strength of rule comes from educated leaders, that there should be a loyal acceptance of the difference
between leaders and citizens, and that the highest reward of a
citizen is to be asked to join the government. That Li Qin is
a member of the Communist Youth League answers the question of how she made her way to Columbia University; it also
explains why the party continues to support her company with
the encouragement of various subsidies.

China's talent advances up the government ladder step
by step and with a long-term view. Young party leaders are
expected to acquire operational experience before aspiring
to political positions, and ministers are required to work in

China's poorest provinces before being considered for higher posts within the central government.

China's current president, Xi Jinping, is a "princeling," the son of a senior party member. But it must be noted that Xi has risen methodically through China's political ranks over time, serving first as the governor of Fujian Province and then as the governor and Communist Party of China chief of neighboring Zhejiang. Xi was deliberately transferred to Shanghai to become a party secretary in advance of his move to the central government, where he was groomed for several years as Hu Jintao's successor. Having completed an arduous political process before assuming the presidential mantle he would wear for ten years, Xi Jinping might question just how much American presidents can realistically accomplish during their maximum eight-year tenures, particularly when getting reelected becomes a distraction midcourse.

America continues to argue—less and less convincingly—that a one-person, one-vote version of democracy should be the world's role model. China has already proved that a one-party system can deliver dynamic economic growth. It seems to me that whether or not China eventually gravitates toward some incremental version of democracy, what will secure its future is its single-voiced narrative. That underlying unity has been China's inner cohesion and explains the astonishing determination of its people.

Defining themselves in varying cycles of money and power, dynasties are the milestones of Chinese history. Since some dynasties are disputed by historians to be mythological, and others are considered sub-dynasties, it is difficult to say precisely how many dynasties China has had. General agreement puts it at no fewer than nineteen.

The history of America has yet to run the length of a single, three-hundred year Chinese dynasty, giving credence to the suggestion that China is playing chess while America plays checkers. History will remember which game is more meaningful, but history takes time.

Meanwhile, China is exporting itself in very large numbers.

CHAPTER THIRTY

With the ever-increasing number of Chinese working outside of China, my editor wanted me to write a chapter on how to behave in foreign business settings.

I began with job interviews.

→ *LESSON 22*

Etiquette is what happens when two people come into contact and interact—which has everything to do with looking for and securing a job. Seeking employment requires you to meet people you don't know, to communicate your skills, and to prove that you not only have the wherewithal to do the job but are also a pleasant person to be around.

Keep in mind that as soon as you open your mouth to speak, the person listening to you is subconsciously judging your ability to be understood. There is a natural bond between what you say and how you say it. That correlation is important to keep in mind. Your voice should serve the meaning of what you are saying and the circumstances in which you are saying it. If you are being interviewed for a job, your voice should be strong (which is not to say it should be loud) and controlled. It should be forceful on the points you wish to emphasize. If you are talking to someone who is conveying bad news, never giggle or laugh, no matter how uncomfortable or nervous you are. It is considered a rude and insensitive reaction by Westerners.

Here is some advice on how to achieve a pleasant speaking voice:

· Do not speak too loudly. To Westerners, a loud voice is thought to indicate aggression and anger, so remember to bring your voice down a notch or two.
· Try not to speak in a monotone. It flattens Westerners' interest.
· Your voice should sound enthusiastic, not depressed.
· Try not to speak too fast. Fast talkers are more difficult to understand and often have to repeat themselves.
· Don't swallow your words—enunciate.
· Don't worry about your accent. That you are speaking English is an achievement.

→ *LESSON 23*

During a job interview, be sure to look the person who is interviewing you in the eye. Do not have a frown on your face. It looks as if you are in a bad mood. Do not fold your arms tightly in front of you or turn away from the person who is speaking. Don't fidget or continually shift positions in your chair. It looks as if you are not paying attention. Men, do not pick at your nails while listening; women, don't study your manicure while listening. It indicates indifference. Never look at your watch, which implies you can't wait to get away from the person who is speaking. Your last comment before ending the interview should be that you are a hard worker and a problem solver and that you work well with other people.

Just as they are not particularly comfortable with hellos, the Chinese do not partake in drawn-out good-byes. Often it has been the case that my Chinese colleagues abruptly take their leave at the end of a meal, having exchanged business cards before they were seated. I added my warning against this: "Westerners believe the handshake concluding a meeting is just as important as the one that introduced you. Do not rush away."

Given the sometimes confusing matter of what, exactly, constitutes right and wrong behavior between men and women in Western workplaces, I thought I should include advice on those issues as well.

→ *LESSON 24*

A woman cannot change the attitude of an obtuse man who has a preconceived notion of the opposite gender, but she *can* hold him responsible for maintaining a professional demeanor, and that is precisely what she must do. Sexual harassment is defined in various ways, but two clear markers are conduct that creates a hostile work environment and a promotion or firing that results from an employee's submission to or rejection of sexual advances or overtures.

Most companies are vague on the issue of personal relationships in the office. But common sense dictates that if there is a mutual attraction, both the man and the woman should inquire if their company has a specific policy about dating superiors or subordinates. It is a slippery slope if either the man or the woman has the authority to promote or demote the other.

Just as a woman bears a burden of behavior in the workplace, so too does a man. More than before, men are held accountable for inappropriate behavior in the office, regardless of whether a woman encourages that behavior. Men, you might keep in mind that there is a larger truth about men and women. Generally speaking, your views of intimacy or sexuality are very different from most women's. It is up to you to act against the moment and to remind yourself of the implications if you force your attentions on a female coworker. Err on the side of caution, and if there is any question about how to behave, head for the higher ground and look toward common sense. Both are located above your waist.

After I sent my editor the chapter, he phoned to tell me that he wanted more lessons on working outside of China. That's what I assumed he wanted. It was difficult to tell. The day he phoned was the day he decided to practice his English.

Chinese who have studied English since elementary school can recite grammar. They have memorized the rules of conjugation. They can understand complicated written texts. What they often cannot do is assemble complete sentences that are not prefabricated.

"Your passport need copy," was what he told me.

"Do you mean you need to copy my passport?" I asked. "Is there a problem? I've already given you a copy of my passport."

"No problem."

Then he took back some part of his answer.

"Only *small* problem," he said.

"What kind of small problem?"

"Tomorrow go to lunch."

"Should I worry?" I asked, but he had already hung up.

The recurring issue of my passport didn't frighten me, but it dilated my apprehension and put me in an ongoing state of pre-fear.

"You live many places," announced the editor as we sat down for lunch the next day. "Too many stamps on top your passport."

I'm not sure how many places are too many, but it is true that I had lived in several other places before Beijing. Apparently, the number of them strained credibility with the Chinese authorities. On the other hand, the fact that I had successfully navigated such uncharted foreignness put me in high esteem with my editor. Having seen the French *carte de séjour* in my passport, he wanted to hear the details of the year—many years ago—I lived in Paris, a place he had only read about.

Out of politeness, and because he was so very eager to hear about Paris, I shared what I could remember of my life there.

IN 1998, NEARLY ten years after *Buzz* was launched in L.A., the Fairchild Corporation purchased it. Despite the magazine's sale, our household required two incomes; mine was the financial anchor. Worry about what would be next for us consumed most of my waking—and many of what should have been my sleeping—hours.

W. had a more relaxed attitude. He wasn't the least bit uncomfortable when there appeared a deficit between life's expenditures and its earnings. His charmed life owed a transparent debt to luck, which he was in no rush to repay. I was the reality-wedded party in our marriage. I was the one who insisted on a plan.

When all was said and done, whatever plans I'd outlined, whatever options I'd proposed for the immediate future, were not as interesting as the unscripted adventure W. presented one afternoon.

"I ran into someone I know who knows a French family that wants to spend a school year in New York," was how it blithely began.

"Yes . . . ?" I asked tentatively.

"They're three of them: parents and a boy Gilliam's age. He'd be going to the lycée."

"And?"

"And we should consider swapping apartments with them."

"It's late July," I pointed out. "School begins in another month. It's too rushed a plan."

"You could use the break, and this is probably the only way we could afford it. Besides, there's no difference between the lycée program here and the one Gilly would have in Paris."

W. had managed to back into the truth.

It turned out the French couple couldn't swap apartments,

but they were keen to sublet ours. And because ours came fully furnished, we were in a position to charge considerably more than we were paying in rent—enough to afford an apartment in Paris, enough to supplement my much-needed sabbatical. W. would continue to draw cartoons for *The New Yorker* and write. Both could be done from Paris.

As for me, I savored the idea of an experience not yet had: staying at home. I would become fluent in French. I would discover a beautiful city. I would allow myself the time to be curious. I would be happy.

That was my plan.

It is said that if you want to make the gods laugh, tell them your plans.

No part of my plan actually happened, though it looked as if it might. We rented an apartment on the shuttered, balconied Boulevard Suchet, situated in a residential section of the Sixteenth Arrondissement called Auteuil, known for its old-fashioned elegance and reputable public school.

Gilliam was entering fifth grade, and for the first time in his life my routine was set to his day. Our morning walk to school took us through the local marketplace, where women and men alike would scrutinize tomatoes and ask detail-oriented questions about the mushrooms—a demographically equal testament to how seriously the French take their food.

On the ground floor of Gilliam's lycée lived an elderly concierge. She kept a pair of caged parakeets in the lobby, and at precisely eight o'clock the front door was opened wide enough for her dog to rush out and relieve himself against the nearby tree. A moment later, Madame Concierge would appear to post the lunch menu and welcome the children.

Human identities are made of malleable material, and we can change according to where we are. It is especially so with children. Gilliam became French in habit almost immediately. His breakfast converted to a small baguette dunked in a bowl of hot chocolate, and he acquired the existential French shrug, conveyed with a downward mouth and the open-ended comment-without-comment *Bah, alors.*

Nothing remotely French rubbed off on me. It wasn't given

the chance. In fact, all but one aspect of my plan for Paris disappeared after I unpacked our bags. I received a unique job offer from the Hearst Corporation a few weeks after arriving in Paris, which derailed my sabbatical. But it doesn't take long to be happy there, and that part of my plan was what actually happened. In the limited time I was in Paris, I was happy because, quite simply, Paris is a place that delivers happiness in a way that has nothing to do with advancement and everything to do with transformation.

As impolite as the French sometimes appear, I respect them for their belief that their culture is worth constant care; I admire the curatorial devotion they have toward it; and I like the fact that they make a point of upholding high standards of comportment.

"God would be perfectly happy in France," wrote Saul Bellow after he experienced Paris for the first time, "because he would not be troubled by prayers, observances, blessings and demands for the interpretation of difficult dietary questions. Surrounded by unbelievers He too could relax toward evening, just as thousands of Parisians do at their favorite cafes."

The number of Chinese people who live outside mainland China surpasses the number of French people living in France. Still, it was difficult for me to imagine a Frenchman relaxing at a café conversing with someone other than another Frenchman or God, so when the editor asked for an additional lesson on business politesse outside of China, I did not place it in France. Instead, I followed China's money to the United Arab Emirates, where some two thousand Chinese firms operate.

→ *LESSON 25*

Virtually all Arab nations adhere to the Muslim religion, and etiquette in these countries is largely based on the observance of the Koran.

Here are some basic points:
· Men, shake hands with only men. Do not offer your hand to a woman.

· Wear only long pants if you are a man, and long pants or a long skirt if you are a woman.

· If you are a woman, you must cover your arms, so wear long sleeves.

· When you are seated, keep both feet on the floor and don't show the soles of your shoes. It is seen as a sign of disrespect.

· Don't touch anyone on the head, which is considered sacred.

· Don't ever ask your host's wife for news of the family, for the host may have several wives. Better to ask, "How is your household?"

· If you are traveling with your wife, refrain from any display of affection in public.

· The Koran forbids a woman to reveal a great deal of her physical self, starting with the crown of her head. Do not ask about that custom, and do not stare.

· When visiting a mosque, remove your shoes before entering and leave them outside.

· Do not cross in front of someone who is in prayer.

· Do not touch food with the left hand, which is considered impure.

· When entering your host's home, step into it with your right foot.

· Alcohol is never consumed, nor is pork.

· The practice of hospitality is all-important. If you are entertaining an Arab in your home, you must give the impression of abundance. If you are eating in the home of an Arab, do not volunteer your admiration of any possession of his, for it will become yours.

· When giving gifts, keep in mind that Islam prohibits the reproduction of the human face.

Like a small but deadly time bomb, one word in this written lesson would prevent my book from being published the month it was scheduled to appear in stores.

PART ELEVEN

Raising Sons

清官难断家务事.

Easier to rule a nation than a son.

—*Chinese proverb*

CHAPTER THIRTY-ONE

Though China's Communist Party has recently agreed to a less draconian approach, its one-child policy will not be entirely forsaken anytime soon, for it is meant to slow the drain on the country's resources. The result is a nation of predominately sibling-free children who are the future of their country and the source of their parents' security.

While other cultures seem to be dispensing with the idea of family, family ties in China remain at the center of its value system, and children are treated like precious cargo. But there is a price for being so cherished. From an early age, Chinese children are expected to fulfill responsibilities to their parents—responsibilities laid out clearly in a code of conduct issued by China's National Committee on Aging. It incorporates the themes of *The Twenty-Four Paragons of Filial Piety*, written during the Yuan dynasty in the late 1200s. I made a gift of the book to Gilliam. Just as the title promises, it features twenty-four stories demonstrating exemplary acts. One tale tells of a son who lies down naked on a frozen river so the ice will melt, allowing him to catch fish for his father—a particularly ludicrous display of stupidity all around, suggested my own son.

Given the belief by the Chinese that their ancestors merge into the forces of the universe, given, as well, the more earthbound issue of succession, particularly when it comes to family-owned businesses and newly built empires, and given China's one-child policy—given all of these things, it is no surprise that in China the urge to have sons is now skewing the gender balance of the population.

Increasingly and for the next twenty years, China will have more men than women of reproductive age. That has prompted the government to openly express concern about the consequences the gender imbalance will have on the nation's social stability.

Thousands of years before the ancient lessons of *The Twenty-Four Paragons of Filial Piety*, Egyptians set forth *The Instruction of Ptahhotep*, a collection of maxims that sowed the seeds of Western ethical conduct.

"How worthy it is when a son hearkens to his father . . . and how many misfortunes befall him who hearkens not!" cautions Ptahhotep.

I cannot help wondering if what resides not far below the surface of his warning is the primal fear of fathers that their sons will surpass them. Though never a great fan of Freud, I have seen for myself how accurate is his timeline charting the early childhood development of boys.

Gilliam went to sleep one night a four-year-old devoted to both of his parents and woke the next morning determined to eliminate his father in order to have his mother to himself. Before breakfast, he walked purposefully into the next room and glared at his competition stationed at a desk, drawing cartoons.

His father looked up.

"Well, hello, Gilly. Have you come to visit? How nice."

Gilliam's intentions were expressed politely, but they were as deadly serious as a Russian oligarch.

"You need to move out of our house," he announced.

Caught off guard, his father nonetheless managed to retain the convincing tone of adult authority.

"This is my house as well," he reminded his son.

Gilliam considered the accuracy of his father's statement. Unhappily, it was correct.

"You wouldn't have to go far," Gilliam suggested.

"Where would you have me go?" asked his father with amused curiosity.

"What about the garage? That way you could visit," Gilliam reasoned.

In China, it could well be that the cultural factors of Confucianism would have made the kind of Oedipal exchange between Gilliam and his father unnecessary. Perhaps far more thought provoking is the ever-increasing number of young Chinese men. By 2020, China expects a surplus of thirty-five million of them. That number of males for whom there will be no available women in China exceeds the entire population of Canada. This will not happiness make.

On the other hand, I'm not entirely sure what kind of happiness is actively encouraged in China, other than the kind that rewards achievement.

Instilled in the Chinese by the Cultural Revolution was the belief that pursuing happiness at the expense of others ran contradictory to the moral principle of communism and therefore those who did so would never be happy. The idea of romantic love has been systematically dismissed by Chinese politics as both frivolous and selfish. Perhaps it is a blessing in disguise. With so little reference made to romantic love, most likely Chinese people have been spared the anguish of its loss.

East or West, we are never entirely honest when it comes to issues of love, and so it is doubtful I can be the reliable narrator of my own. I am, however, absolutely certain that I married W. for love.

"For better or for worse" were words in a vow I took completely to heart. Fifteen years later, my heart remained devoted, but it was physically, emotionally, and financially impossible to continue life as it was. I hoped I could make W. understand this. Instead, he pivoted in an entirely different direction.

Despite my profound dislocation, I was determined to create security for Gilliam. *Security is home,* I reasoned. *I will make our home safe,* I told myself. Safety, at least the reassuring illusion of it, is to be found in a household routine, and so Gilliam and I became an enterprise of sorts, with the shared responsibility of routine. Each morning after breakfast, I left for the office and Gilliam left for school. Each night during dinner, we compared our days and made plans for the next . . . each night, a plan for the following day . . . and the following, and the following . . . until, gradually, sadness lost its place and possibilities appeared in front of me. Isak Dinesen once said that sorrows can be borne if you put them in a story. I did that. I wrote a novel.

My life was uncommonly full, as was Gilliam's. But the unspoken circumstances that reduced us from a tight three-person family to only mother and son required of me a sustained effort to redirect our futures, both of which had been pushed off course. I decided we should travel.

Regardless of where our journeys took us, I packed no more than could be carried on the plane. We were efficiency in motion, but the frantic hour before leaving was a showcase of my least attractive qualities. It took only a few trips for Gilliam to recognize my pretrip irrationality. He would station himself near the front door, away from the dangerous whirl of my helicopter blades.

If a psychiatrist were to explain that my anxiety had nothing to do with getting to the airport on time, he would not be telling me anything I did not already know. I understood the reason behind my pretravel angst: I was responsible for Gilliam's life, but no one was sheltering mine. That fear made its own place, filled with longing and self-pity. Guilt lived there too—guilt for feeling anything other than gratitude that my son and I were fortunate in our health, that we were buffered by my resourcefulness, and that we both lived advantaged lives.

Determined not to allow my emotions to take the lead, I called on my organizational skills to hold them back. There were prerequisites to our trips. The flight was nonstop and overnight Thursday, placing us in the foreign city on Friday morning. By sleeping on the plane, we were able to stay in the local time zone for the two days we explored the city. We left on Sunday, the time difference returning us to New York before dinner. Slightly longer trips coincided with Gilliam's French holidays, when off-season travel made it possible for me to afford more than our usual two-night stay.

Varied and vivid and surprising, our trips offered as many reasons for taking them as there were places to go. Sufis and Agatha Christie were two good reasons for Istanbul. The Goya exhibit at the Prado lured us to Madrid. A loaned apartment on the Île Saint-Louis made Paris possible. Mozart's *Magic Flute* was the excuse for Vienna. Pompeian frescoes and the Cappella Sansevero's *Veiled Christ* waited for us in Naples.

Three holidays anchored us to the same places with our offbeat version of an extended family: the Fourth of July was in Capri with the same set of friends from L.A.; Thanksgiving had a counterintuitive place in London with Gilliam's English godmother and her family; Christmas Eve dinner was celebrated with a boisterous group of New Yorkers. Our birthdays—two days apart in August—were spent in foreign cities we'd not yet visited.

Gilliam's life took shape in cities: L.A. was where he grew out of his infancy; Paris claimed some part of his childhood; New York—a city of sharp corners and brute force—seemed an appropriate backdrop for the assertive male pride of his adolescence.

Raising a son on my own confirmed what I long ago suspected: men and women are not set apart by biology; they *are* biology. The dissolution of my marriage left me with full-time parental responsibilities for Gilliam, and I carried the financial obligations of that unforgiving fact. Gilliam respected my role in our household, and I appreciated his. That was before, at the age of fourteen, he mutated into something unrecognizable.

Surliness appeared for the first time and fed defiance; defiance egged on provocation, until life with my son became like handling nitroglycerin. Expecting anything from Gilliam on the weekends became his equivalent of a miscarriage of justice. At first, I was furious at what I believed to be his indolence, but then I became worried when he slept for long stretches.

"Does he nod off in the middle of activities?" asked our doctor after I insisted Gilliam must be suffering from narcolepsy.

"There *are* no activities on the weekend—unless you consider eating to be one," I told him. "The boy eats constantly when he's not sleeping. I don't understand that either because he's so thin. Could he have picked up a tapeworm on one of our trips?"

Ignoring my question, the doctor asked one of his own. "What about school, does he fall asleep in class?"

"No. He's fine in school. It's the weekends that are lost."

"It's not lost time if it's spent sleeping," the doctor pointed out.

"Of course you're right," I said, not because I agreed but because I wanted to sound supportive.

"The thing is, no matter how much sleep Gilliam has, he's exhausted. Do you think he has caught one of those sleeping diseases you get from parasitically infected third-world water?" I asked.

"Your son doesn't have a tapeworm or a sleeping disease," said the doctor.

"Then what *does* he have?"

"He doesn't 'have' anything. The boy is growing."

I would not argue with that point. Gilliam's height had increased five inches that year alone.

"All right," I told the doctor. "I'll let the boy grow."

And so Gilliam's weekends remained forty-eight-hour rotations of sleeping, eating, lounging, and standing—mutely and without purpose—in front of the open refrigerator. The few times he was actually in motion, his behavior was recklessly driven by his glands.

"Any suggestion of mine is a detonation device," I complained to Annie.

"Testosterone," was all she said.

I waited for more.

"It's been shown that the increase of testosterone causes certain species to patrol larger areas so they can pick more fights," explained Annie.

Actually, that sounded familiar. When he wasn't manufacturing a crisis, Gilliam would search me out, reach into the inner chamber of his psyche, and select a poison dart tipped with the most hurtful thing to say. So precise was the boy's cunning bull's-eye aim that it took a single accusation to hit the very core of my defenselessly open maternal heart.

Gilliam's increasingly provocative attitude was not unlike that of his favorite childhood character, the atrociously behaved Monkey King.

DESPITE THE IMPORTANCE of deference in Chinese culture, one of the most enduring Chinese literary characters is Sun Wukong, also known as Monkey King, whose egotistical and prankish misbehavior was put to paper by Wu Cheng'en in the sixteenth-century epic novel *Journey to the West*.

It begins, logically enough, with the beginning of time.

Born from a stone is a monkey with supernatural powers but very little sense of propriety. His acts of destruction and disrespect against, among others, the Ocean Dragons and the God of Death came to the attention of the august Ruler of the Universe, the Jade Emperor. A diplomat first and foremost, the Jade Emperor invited Monkey King to heaven and—believing it would placate him—bestowed on him the double-barreled title of Great Sage, Equal of Heaven. But the incorrigible Monkey King went on a spree of mythically proportioned bad behavior. He gate-crashed a party meant for the officials of heaven, where he ate all of the prized Longevity Pills, stuffed his face with Peaches of Immortality, and—before fleeing heaven in a single bound—taunted the Jade Emperor with an obscene gesture recognized by mortals and gods alike.

When the Jade Emperor sent his Heavenly Army after Monkey King, it was defeated by his wickedly clever tricks and overwhelming powers. Realizing that any attempt to subdue Monkey King by force would prove fruitless, Buddha made a wager with him. If Monkey King could jump off the palm of Buddha's hand, Buddha would demote Jade Emperor and Heaven would fall under Monkey King's jurisdiction. If, however, Monkey King was unable to leap the distance, an apology would be expected and a severe and long penance would be due. Knowing himself to be capable of leaping thousands of miles at a time, Monkey King quickly agreed to the bargain.

Buddha stretched out his hand.

Monkey King's jump landed him thousands of miles away in a desolate plain with five great columns reaching to the sky. *These must be the Five Pillars of Wisdom at the end of the Universe,* he thought. And in a vulgar display of territorial imperative, Monkey King urinated against the nearest pillar before leaping back into Buddha's palm to claim his right to Heaven.

Raising a sublime eyebrow, Buddha informed an astonished Monkey King that although the leap could indeed be measured in thousands of miles, Monkey King had not in fact left Buddha's palm. Worse news was that the pillars were Buddha's fingers, one of which had been defiled. Monkey King was banished by Buddha, who trapped him under a mountain until Monkey King agreed to make peace with the universe.

CLOSER TO HOME, reason and determination—two attributes that served me in my professional life—worked against me with my son. *Either I come up with a plan,* I told myself, *or one of us will end up killing the other.*

What saved us both was not so much a plan but a different approach: I let go of control. Despite his taciturn determination to operate in perversely oppositional terms, Gilliam acknowledged my gesture. The boy-man told me he loved me dearly. He told me he admired me greatly. He told me he was incredibly thankful for me. He told me he intended to go to Japan and learn the language.

At the time, my son was seventeen. The rarefied life we shared had come to its rightful end.

THERE WERE TWO things to be done before Gilliam left for Japan.

The first—my idea, not his—was a serious discussion about

the differences between Asian and Western attitudes toward intimate relationships. I felt it my obligation as a stand-in father to have this conversation with Gilliam before he left. By no means was I comfortable with the subject. I am a fairly private person and, admittedly, old-fashioned in my views. The last and only time I had spoken to my son about sex was when he was five and he insisted I explain human reproduction.

"So, tell me," Candida asked at the time, "how do you discuss sex with a five-year-old?"

"The books I've read suggest I tell him in words he can understand."

"You'll never get anywhere that way," she said. "Try finding one of those intrauterine films. It's the perfect solution. The entire subject of sex has been scientifically dry-cleaned, and there's no need to say anything. You just watch the film with him."

The following week, Gilliam sat on the couch expectantly facing the television while I pushed the PLAY button. On the screen appeared sperm as seen through an electron microscope, a thousand times their actual size.

I addressed the obvious first. "Of course they're infinitely smaller," I said as my son and I watched a menacing number of diabolically large sperm swarm before our eyes.

"There're so many," was Gilliam's initial reaction.

"That's right," I said, trying to keep to the script. "And do you see that they are all moving in one direction?"

"No . . ."

He was right again. It was bedlam. Bumper-car-size sperm were darting erratically from side to side, careening into one another before finally finding their collective sense of direction. The longer Gilliam watched them struggle upstream, the more worried he became. When the one sperm had reached the single egg, he asked me to stop the tape.

"But, sweetie, the film isn't finished yet," I said.

"Can you rewind it? I want to see the beginning. I don't care about who gets there first. I want to see what happens to the others."

Gilliam's intense focus was on the journey of the sperm,

not their destination. He insisted we watch the first few minutes of the film over again several times. We never got to the fertilized egg.

"The rest of the sperm are absorbed into the mother's bloodstream," I explained when he asked what became of them.

I knew that hundreds of redundant sperm had a far less dignified ending but decided to recast it in an optimistic cycle-of-life message.

"You mean they die," said Gilliam.

"No, they become something else."

"So what is it that they become?" asked my son, clearly onto me.

"Well, they . . . I think they . . . ," I stuttered.

Gilliam put an end to my instructional failure. "The truth is they die," he said matter-of-factly. "They die for one life to be possible."

Unable as I was then to deal with the boy's metaphorical take on the subject, how was I now to address the more subtle issue of what I considered his obligations as a young man when it came to young women in Asia, a place where—once intimacy takes place—the cultural expectations are decidedly different?

"You can't afford to get this wrong," warned Jonathan. "You'll ruin it for him for the rest of his life."

"Ruin what?" I asked.

"Everything," he told me.

It was then that I decided I would write a letter to Gilliam instead and surreptitiously pack it with the belongings he would take to Japan.

Fortunately, the second obligation requiring my attention before Gilliam left home was an easier proposition.

PART TWELVE

A Series of Departures

及时行乐.

Enjoy yourself—it's later than you think.
—*Chinese proverb*

CHAPTER THIRTY-TWO

It was the last year of my almost ten-year tenure at Hearst. The phone call came to my office.

"It's me," he said without announcing himself.

"Greg?"

He lowered his voice so it was barely audible.

"Have I missed the Turtle Release?"

"No. You haven't missed it."

"Thank God I have *something* to look forward to."

"Where are you?"

"I'm here."

"As in New York here?"

"Lon . . ."

"Did you say London?"

"That's right, *goddamn it,* London," he complained. The unseen but damnable "it" hammered his impatience into a thin wedge of anger.

"I assume whatever's going on isn't going very well," I said.

His response was garbled.

"It sounds like you're talking through a wet towel," I told him. "I can barely hear you."

"I'm talking as loud as I can under the circumstances."

"Are you okay?"

"As a matter of fact, I am *not* okay. What I am is stuck in the middle of a negotiation taking longer than anyone bloody well expected."

"You haven't missed it," I repeated.

"Have the invitations gone out?" he asked.

"No."

"So I assume the shipment isn't in."

"Not yet."

"Do you think they'll show up by the end of the month?"

"I doubt it."

"Why not?"

"Because they're coming from some godforsaken part of Asia."

"I thought they arrived the same time every year," he persisted.

"Yes . . . usually when the weather turns warm."

"Well?"

"Well, what?"

"It was warm when I left New York a few weeks ago."

"Not any longer," I pointed out. "It's cold now."

"Goddamn it," was his refrain.

"Greg, listen, I can't do anything about the weather or the shipment."

"I realize that," he said in a slightly more conciliatory tone. "I want to be there. . . . I plan to be there. . . ."

"If it's any help, we've always done it on a Tuesday or Wednesday," I offered.

"I remember . . . in the middle of the week, when fewer people are around . . . after hours."

The man on the phone was a friend and the president of a large publicly traded company. When our conversation took place, big business was at low tide ethically. Even under the best of circumstances, our cryptic exchange would have made us sound guilty of something: references to "shipment" and "after hours" suggested an illegal transaction; the item in question was arriving from Asia, adding a sinisterly global reach. If investigators from the Securities and Exchange Commission questioned us, we'd have to admit the facts: the Turtle Release was an annual event, the date of which was impossible to schedule in advance. It took place in public spaces, but was shrouded by ceremonial secrecy.

Two months before Gilliam left for Japan, Greg received what he was waiting for.

The Pleasure of Your Company Is Requested
at
the Final Turtle Release
Tuesday, April 2nd
17 East 95th Street
5:30 p.m. Champagne
&

7:00 p.m. Release
Central Park Pond
(a short walk from the apartment)

A Chinatown is a micrometropolis that operates with an enduring distrust of the outside world, no matter which international city acts as its backdrop. The Chinese make a single-ingredient bouillabaisse from turtles, believing they impart longevity. It was customary—or so we concluded from years of personal experience—that red-eared sliders were shipped seasonally from Asia. That particular year in New York, the turtles arrived the last week of March. Though fishmongers in New York's Chinatown are easily found, turtles are not. Down a narrow side lane . . . in an open-air fish stand . . . under a large tray of eels . . . there they were: turtles stacked in a deep wooden barrel.

Handicapped by my tendency to anthropomorphize, I was hopelessly emotional when it came to the actual selection; Gilliam decided which one of the turtles to rescue. Instructing me to stand a respectable distance away, he made his choice with unsparing objectivity.

Because it was impossible to know the precise date the turtles would arrive in Chinatown, there was, inevitably, a period of waiting between the time the rescue occurred and the time the release took place. After taxiing uptown with the chosen turtle, we hosed it off in Gilliam's bathtub. During a week of sanctioned luxury, the turtle lounged in its tub, dined on straw-berries, and wandered among the claw-feet of the nineteenth-century furniture in our living room.

Turtle Releases in New York were traditionally scheduled on weekday evenings, when there were fewer people in Central Park, for truth be told, we were breaking the law—or, at the very least, ignoring the warning posted in front of the pond. Given our need to accomplish the actual release as quickly as possible, its celebration occurred at a reception beforehand. Among those marking the occasion were actors, authors, and musicians. Seduced by an available audience, encouraged by the champagne, they recited verse, played ditties on the piano, and offered toasts before we set off for the park.

A large sign in front of the pond forbidding the introduc-tion of any other reptiles made it difficult to disregard the Asian embarkation of what we intended to set free. The law-abiding part of me worried someone would report us to the authorities, and I scanned the area furtively before approach-ing. There—waiting in the designated area—was Greg, having come directly from the airport in time to watch the last in a decade of turtles lumber purposely toward its freedom.

Ten years. Ten turtles transported across continents and chosen by the luck of the draw to be returned to whatever nature was available in the middle of whichever city we were living in at the time. For Gilliam, the turtles counted down the annual passing of his boyhood. For me, they were the unlikely markers mapping a journey through what was then an unexplored—and what is now an unforgettable—decade of our lives.

CHAPTER THIRTY-THREE

The year of the last Turtle Release was the year I began to measure what it was costing me to preserve my self-sufficiency.

"I'm not very good at this anymore," I told Jonathan.

"Good at what?"

"Being alone."

"You have suitors," Jonathan was kind to remind me. "The problem is they're all peculiar," he added.

"They are *not* all peculiar," I insisted. "Well . . . not all of them."

"Who are you trying to kid? My favorite is the one who eats paper."

"He is a brilliant thinker," was my defense of the man who—it is true—ate paper.

"Then there's the one from the ancient European family who cuts the tops off his socks. And what about the Brit?"

"Peter?"

"He's obviously working for MI6."

"Why would you say that?"

"Because he's an Englishman of a certain age who went to Oxford at a time when it was an absolute breeding ground for them. He doesn't seem to live anywhere. No one understands what he does, and he seems to have memorized the train schedules in Eastern Europe. He's a spy. Think about it."

Before I could think about it, Jonathan warned me off

someone we both knew who had a well-earned reputation for promiscuity.

"He must be a viral minefield by now," I said.

"His wife has finally kicked him out," said Jonathan.

"I remember her at our reception for Gilliam's christening. She spent the entire time in our kitchen sobbing," I said. "But that's almost, what, twenty years ago? How has she put up with the situation for this long?"

"With pharmaceuticals, I should think," said Jonathan before asking, "What about Coco? He's eccentric enough to appeal to you."

Coco was a notorious renegade, tempestuous and mercurial, habitually late for everyone and everything. He was also wonderfully fascinating. "We'll make a plan" was an expression of his I came to love. Unlike my own results-oriented plans, his had no other purpose than a good time. Coco was never a suitor. We never made a plan. Not because I thought he was unacceptable, though he could be. Not because he was impossible; I forgave him for that. But because, by the time we met, he was dying.

Even in death, Chinese parents project themselves into the lives of their children, whose unquestioned devotion assigns the obligation of arranging funerals for their elders. When, during my first week in Dongzhimen, I came upon the young man begging for money to bury his mother, it was not only grief I saw in his eyes, but fear of not being able to do what was expected of him. In circumstances less desperate, most funerals are scheduled—much like weddings—after consulting the Chinese almanac for the best possible dates. White is the color reserved for death, and so white invitations are sent, unless the deceased was eighty years or older, in which case the invitations are pink, an acknowledgment that mourners are expected to celebrate the person's longevity rather than mourn his or her passing. All beyond death is regarded as dark, and it is believed that by lighting candles at the funeral, the dead are made to see how and where to go.

White envelopes filled with cash—much like the red envelopes given at weddings—are left for the family near the wreath of the deceased. The amount placed in each envelope varies according to the giver's relationship with the deceased but must be an odd number. Just as money is of practical importance in the here and now, so, too, in the afterlife. During the burial ceremony, the family burns paper money as a wire transfer of sorts so there will be no financial concerns for the deceased upon arriving in the afterworld.

Unquestionably, best prepared for whatever his afterlife would entail was China's first emperor, Qin Shihung, who took up arms at the age of thirteen to unify the warring Asian tribes and died at the age of forty-six. Buried with him is a larger-than-life three-thousand-man army precisely and individually replicated in ceramic. Soldiers and generals, along with their horses, were discovered in perfect formation in fortified underground tombs—tombs so skillfully hidden that they remained unearthed in Xi'an until the 1970s.

The tombs are staggering proof of China's cultural sophistication two hundred years before Christ—which was what I was contemplating when I emerged from these ancient underground wonders into broad daylight to find that the only exit was through the gift shop.

There in the gift shop—a gift shop looking not unlike any other museum shop in the West—was the farmer who, some forty years earlier, had discovered the tombs while digging for water on land dispossessed during the Cultural Revolution. He appeared to me the embodiment of modern China, sitting comfortably behind a desk and charging tourists for his autograph.

THE YEAR OF the last Turtle Release was also the year Candida was dying of cancer.

"Don't be sad," she told me. "I've had a good run."

"How bad is the pain?" I asked.

"Agonizing. But the good news is I'll finally meet the Jew-God," she told me.

Given the relatively short time one has to make sense of

life, the outcome of death seems unfair, and in the aspiration of making sense of our finite existence, most of us look for comfort in what we believe is the answer to life's infinitely unknowable questions. Jew-God, Buddha, Shiva—the name for that answer makes little difference. Laozi, a Chinese philosopher who is traditionally credited with founding Taoism in the sixth century B.C., described his metaphysical search in resolutely modern words.

> *Once something arose out of non-existence before Heaven and Earth and came into being. . . . It softens asperity, unravels complexity, moderates effulgence, co-ordinates particles. Invisible, yet real, I know not whose son it is, but it precedes the sovereign stars.*

"Before you meet your Maker, what should we do?" I asked Candida when the pain became unbearable for her.

"I have a choice. . . . I could end it," she told me, alluding to a final act of self-determination. "But I'm curious about death. I won't cheat myself out of greeting it when the time comes on its own."

That time came two months later.

Candida was cremated. Her ashes were buried near the trellis behind her house in Stonington, Connecticut. Carving out a cavern above the spot, I reached into my coat pocket, and my hand curled around the moss-green shell I'd found twenty years before on the beach of Africa's Lake Victoria. It was the fragment of a continent to which Candida—the daughter of Italian immigrants—had never been but had wished to see. I put the shell alongside her remains and covered them both with the seaborne earth.

AFTER CANDIDA DIED, time seemed to move in sputtering bursts. Gilliam was one year in Japan, and left for his British university the next. A year later, he left there to live in Nanjing before returning to England once again, this time to complete his degree. My life yo-yoed between Brussels and New York, and work took me from one point on the globe to another. Despite the advantage of a global perspective, I had no idea how humanity would manage its complex future. I was, however, certain on three points. Events in a single location were affecting the world landscape in a matter of moments. Those events were no longer defined, shaped, or resolved primarily by Westerners. And China was fast becoming a game changer. It was that last point that sent me to Beijing with the intention of writing a Western etiquette guide for the Chinese. Three months after I began writing it, I finished with a lesson more contemplative than instructive.

→ *LESSON 26*

Expand your outlook. When you visit someone outside of China or entertain a foreigner in your home, learn about the country of your host or guest. If you are dealing with a colleague from another country, read about that country's current events so you can discuss them knowledgeably; the gesture will indicate the interest you have in him or her. Memorable people always stand out. Look around and take your cue from others you admire. Be generous, be smart about how you handle yourself and others, be interested in learning new things, meeting new people, and traveling to places you have not yet been. These are the important things.

Those who are thriving in what will continue to be a globalized economy are adaptable and persuasive and possess the ability to navigate increasingly diverse cultural landscapes. Comportment has a marketable use: it enables a better understanding of those with different points of view. We are only human, and there is a sometimes overwhelming messiness to that fact. Our complexities and our uncertainties, our personalities and our temperaments—all of these factors unwind in ways that cannot be predicted. Still, we must try to behave with a graceful fortitude, for it is the outward evidence of the best in us.

By early October, *The Tao of Improving Your Likability* was ready for the presses. And I was surrounded by a publishing staff who, with the ferocious speed inherent in the Chinese, took immediate charge of the next crucial phase. Arriving at the front door of my hotel apartment were three young women—all looking the age of girls—and a slightly older-looking young man with an assistant lugging camera equipment.

The young man, who spoke no English, introduced himself by way of his business card: he was a freelance photographer hired by the publisher's production team. One of the three young women—the publisher's marketing director—enlisted her best English while the other two giggled nervously. For what would be the book's front cover, I was instructed to stand with crossed arms in an authoritative pose, looking stern but friendly. After the photographer left, the young woman who spoke English proposed that free scarfs be offered with the book to the first thousand online buyers.

"That will send me down-market," I told the marketing director.

"It's for young women to speak about the book," she said. And by that, I assumed she meant it would generate word of mouth.

The next item of business was tricky. It had to do with registering my own Weibo account. Weibo is the only state-sanctioned social media outlet in mainland China. Once a personal Weibo account is approved by government authorities, a verification badge is added beside the account name.

At the time I was applying to register, some hundred million messages were posted each day on Weibo. In China, self-censorship has become the most effective weapon against action by the state. That is certainly true for foreign news bureaus; they know from experience that they must tread carefully in order to be allowed to continue reporting from China. The Chinese leadership has proved its willingness to punish news organizations that ignore the warning signs, which has led Bloomberg News to employ a system that allows editors to flag postings or articles so that nothing flirting with danger is published in China.

Weibo sets its own strict controls over the posts on its services with a defensive approach that ranges from monitoring users to filtering blacklisted key words. Some users play a dangerous game of communicating in coded languages or writing about their political opinions as allegories. The government's censor has been adept at keeping up with technology. Nearly 30 percent of all deletions occur within five to thirty minutes of posting; 90 percent are completed within twenty-four hours. Offending sites are first blocked and then shut down. It's virtually impossible to reestablish a site once it's closed—the reason even Western media sites are careful to avoid hot-button words. Anything perceived by the party as galvanizing the public sends China's censorship apparatus into an indiscriminate slash-and-burn mentality. At the onset of Tunisia's Jasmine Revolution, the word "jasmine" immediately disappeared from everything in China, including tea.

Despite its tight grip, China's intent is not to shut its people off from the world. It is, however, determined to identify political controversy that threatens to undermine the regime. Unlike the U.S. government—inclined, it seems, to vacuum up wholesale information about citizens and, in so doing, ignore the constitutionally mandated right of privacy—Chinese authorities are motivated to prevent citizens from pursuing a dialogue among themselves.

Social media networks forbidden in China have enabled the voice of a generation to be heard outside of the country. The threat the Internet presents in China is not that it provides information but that it can enable a virtual meeting place. Reacting with silence is the next best thing to agreement, and there is still a great deal of public silence in China. Yet in daily talk, the Chinese discuss thoughts freely among themselves, and like the young man in Tiananmen Square writing on the cement, others of his generation are beginning to openly express themselves.

CHAPTER THIRTY-FOUR

After my Weibo account was successfully registered, everything seemed to be pointing in the right direction.

It wasn't long before Gilliam joined me during his winter break.

We invited a French friend of his—also in Beijing—to help celebrate the holiday. Christmas dinner at one of our favorite restaurants was decidedly un-Christmas-like: tender pieces of white crab in a light, clear soup; emerald-green Chinese broccoli with wedges of roasted garlic; steamed pork dumplings dipped in soy sauce and vinegar; and a succulent duck, its parchment-thin skin cooked to the perfect state of crispness. Made lethargic from the big meal, we decided on a brisk walk back to the hotel.

Beijing's main streets are more like beltways. Called ring roads, they are designated numerically. Currently, there are six of them, with a possible seventh planned.

The origin of the ring roads was the result of the ring-shaped route of the tramlines operating in the 1920s. When the tramlines were removed in the 1950s, the area became a haphazard collection of surface streets, so there is no actual First Ring Road. Beijing's innermost ring road is the Second Ring Road; built in the 1980s and expanded in the 1990s, it passes through the central parts of Beijing. The Third Ring

Road was completed in the 1990s, and the other three have been constructed in the last decade.

Trailing behind Gilliam and his friend on the crowded sidewalk of the Second Ring Road, I struggled to keep pace with their long-limbed strides and was unable to make out their conversation in French. When the three of us were funneled through a busy intersection, Gilliam glanced over his shoulder to make sure I was still there.

It was just then, crossing a Beijing intersection, that I realized that my son's—some would say—nonconformist upbringing had imbued him with a sense of spirited travel, that it had taught him to negotiate the world's cultural differences, and that—at some other moment, in some other place, when I wasn't paying attention—he had charted his own course.

One cannot divine happiness or assign it a location. But as I get older, my own happiness is easier to recognize. It comes unguarded in fleeting, fungible moments when I feel absolutely sure that no other place could grant more happiness than exactly where I am. Seven thousand miles from New York and twelve hours ahead—thirty years after my mother stopped talking to me for reasons known only to her, and ten years after W. left never having said good-bye—I was happy on Christmas Day in China.

THE DAY AFTER Christmas was as bleak as the night before was festive.

Waiting for me at the hotel's front desk was upsetting news. A message from my book editor informed me the censors— after a fine-tooth scrutiny of my book—were withholding permission to publish it. Gilliam stepped in as translator in my meeting with the publisher that afternoon. A single word had caught the eye of the censor: Muslim.

Religions migrate to foreign lands when business is to be found. Since the seventh century, Islam has expanded slowly but methodically across the maritime and inland silk routes.

Muslims have resided in China for fourteen hundred years but are nonetheless considered an ethnic minority. Much like the emotionally charged issue of Tibet, any written reference to Chinese Muslims raises the censor's concern. I had inadvertently wandered into the censor's no-go zone when I included the word in my lesson 25. My word "Muslim" referred not to Chinese Muslims but to Muslims in Arab countries and did not so much as brush up against political implication. It was, quite simply, attached to a friendly, outstretched hand.

But nothing is simple when it comes to the censors in China, and my publishing company had no intention of pushing the issue. They decided to wait it out.

I had no choice but to wait it out with them.

Gilliam returned to England for his next semester. I continued my biweekly trips to Guangzhou to work with Chairman. But circumstances had changed, and now phone calls were made at the security checkpoint in the Beijing airport before I was allowed to board the plane.

"We're more comfortable with paranoia here in China," a Western colleague in China told me, "because it usually turns out to be right."

I didn't know if I was being watched or not. Certainly, my comings and goings were being monitored, and while the authorities were not controlling my activities, my life in China was deliberately circumscribed.

Aware of my plight, Chairman reassured me that I would have no problems in Guangzhou; he proved it by assigning bodyguards to me while I was there. But, instead of reassuring me, Chairman's gesture encouraged an anxious interplay between my imagination and reality. Did he know something I did not? Was I in so much danger while sequestered at Imperial Springs that the bodyguard felt the need to pace up and down the length of the swimming pool, mirroring my morning laps?

Chairman felt he would remove my concerns by suggesting that I work for him on a full-time basis. It was a generous offer, but I had no intention of living in Guangzhou. In fact, I was planning to return to the States after my book was published in China. That being the case, Chairman and I came to an agreement that my consulting services would end no sooner than the Chinese New Year but no later than the Night of a Thousand Lanterns.

The Lantern Festival is celebrated on the fifteenth day of the first month of the traditional Chinese calendar. It is also marked by the first night of the full moon and the end of the two-week Chinese New Year holiday. Since the terms of my contract were pinned to it, I made a point of asking how the festival came to be.

Not unlike other Chinese folktales, this one included a beautiful crane, ignorant mortals, and the angered Jade Emperor—the same Jade Emperor that Monkey King failed to dethrone. It is told that the sacred crane flew from heaven to earth. Whether this was a navigational mistake or a joyride of sorts, I cannot say, but like many poorly planned road trips, it ended badly. The sacred crane—a favorite of the Jade Emperor—was hunted and killed by villagers. The Jade Emperor expressed his outrage by declaring his intention to level the village with a firestorm on the fifteenth lunar day. His daughter warned the inhabitants, and their ruse was to hang red lanterns throughout the village, which created—from the aerial perspective of the gods, one assumes—a false impression that the village was already ablaze.

It would have been easier to assign an end date to my contract with Chairman. But I was in China, after all, and so it would be a full moon that brought my consulting services on his behalf to an end.

PART THIRTEEN

How the Rest Ends

祸兮福所倚, 福兮祸所伏.

A good fortune may forebode a bad luck, which may,
in turn, disguise a good fortune.

—*Chinese proverb*

CHAPTER THIRTY-FIVE

I waited for the censor to release my book. Then I waited some more.

While I waited, I hired David, a young man recently returned to Beijing with a degree from MIT, who agreed to translate my weekly Weibo postings—postings that addressed deportment questions. I also began a series of lectures at Beijing universities on the subject of my book, staying clear of the notorious lesson.

From the lectern, I looked out at packed classrooms of students seated by gender. Many were wearing T-shirts with English slogans that were wrongly translated but, more important, signified modernity. All had in their possession the most recent technological devices so it followed that—with the exception of issues deemed disruptive by the censor—the students were well versed in current events. Leaning forward in their seats, they listened intently to what I had to say, exuding enthusiasm not necessarily for me but for what they imagined I represented.

The Western practice of a question-and-answer session was beached by a collective show of deference. My tactic was to ask the students questions of my own, carefully avoiding the seven banned topics of debate set forth by the state. Shyness gave way to an obvious delight that they were being asked what they thought, and the consensus was that they wanted to follow in the contemporary footsteps of Western culture and to have access to Western branded products. They admired the idea of democracy but pointed out the gulf between democracy's precept and its application. Not all were convinced popular elections would solve China's problems.

If the students had been as free to express their political opinions as openly as they were to express their ambitions, I suspect they would have told me that China's problems are primarily the result of corruption among China's leaders. Since the government is tied closely to all aspects of life in China, and since all aspects of life in China rely to a large degree on *guanxi,* it is not difficult to understand why and how corruption comes into play.

At its worst, *guanxi* undermines the stability of China's central government. That's precisely what happened with Bo Xilai, a former member of the Politburo who is now serving a life sentence, along with his wife, for the poisoning of a British businessman who was once part of her orbit but had made himself into a problem.

In this particular case, there was no need for me to read between the lines of *China Daily.* The party moved into damage-control mode, and the press was swift to turn against Bo. But there was no mention of Chen Guangcheng, the blind civil rights activist known as the "barefoot lawyer," who—while the country remained riveted by the Bo scandal—somehow managed to escape years of house arrest and was ensconced in the American Embassy a few blocks from the St. Regis Hotel.

My work with Chairman had come to an end, and I could do absolutely nothing about the frustrating fact that my book was being held hostage by the Chinese censors. So I decided to return briefly to New York to pay my taxes. That trip spanned less than a week, but that week's events telescoped the issues of China's censorship and illustrated how effectively the Chinese authorities are able to act.

On my way to New York, I stopped in London to see my literary agent, staying the night in Durrants, a hotel so small that there are only three tables in the tea area off its lobby.

I was sitting at one of those three tables during my one

afternoon in London. Seated at the next table, not more than a few feet away, was the artist Ai Weiwei, flanked by two assistants. All three of them were poring over a calendar full of commitments.

When, later, I inquired at the front desk, I was told Ai was in town to install his *Sunflower Seeds* at the Tate Modern. The piece's hundred million life-size sunflower seed husks were handcrafted in porcelain and appear identical but are actually each unique. That night, I made a point of looking at the museum's website. Given what I would soon learn, it would be difficult not to remember the last line of the exhibit's description.

> *Sunflower Seeds invites us to look more closely at the "Made in China" phenomenon and the geo-politics of cultural and economic exchange today.*

In New York the next day, I passed another of his pieces. This one—newly installed around the Pulitzer Fountain in front of the Plaza Hotel—was a series of sculptures, titled *Circle of Animals/Zodiac Heads,* that formed an enormous centerpiece to a multiyear global tour of his work. It came on the heels of his own investigation into and subsequent artistic expression of the shoddy building construction that contributed to the deaths of thousands of schoolchildren during the Sichuan earthquake.

Not long after I had stopped to look at his installation in New York, Ai was surrounded by the Chinese authorities as he was coming through immigration at the Hong Kong airport and taken away.

The grounds for his arrest were never made clear. His own words managed to make themselves heard outside China: "They accused me of five crimes." He was told about only two of them: "inciting subversion of state power" and "economic crimes," which eventually emerged as the tax evasion for which he was publicly condemned and detained another eighty-one days.

This dispiriting news reached me at the airport shortly

before I boarded a plane back to Beijing. I would hear none of it once I arrived there the next day—news of Ai's arrest had already been blocked by the Chinese censor.

Returning to China in its depressingly locked-down frame of mind made almost unbelievable what occurred next.

On June 15, 2011, the censor released my book. Two weeks later, it appeared in stores.

To say that I was incredulous doesn't do justice to what followed. My Weibo account was besieged by comments. Within four weeks, the book became a bestseller in the largest state-owned chain store in mainland China.

The Tao of Improving Your Likability was adopted as a textbook in Peking University's MBA program, and I was asked to write a regular column for the state-sanctioned *China Trade Magazine.* Requests came to address the All-China Women's Federation, to appear at China's elite social clubs, and to lecture at yet more Chinese universities.

This was all happy news, but there was something else going on. In the Weibo offices sat a government official who was closely monitoring my web traffic; my ever-growing following prompted him to act.

David, by then acting as my translator, was notified by the authorities that I should expect a call from them. It was an ominous enough warning for me to contact a trusted Chinese colleague.

"Who is 'them'?" I asked.

" 'Them' is the government," he told me.

Intimidating me further were his instructions: under no circumstances was I to ignore the call when it came.

"That will only make matters worse," he explained.

Convinced I would pay the price for whatever I had done, but completely ignorant of my crime, I could think only of Gilliam's mocking reference to Kafka months before. No longer was it funny.

The call came the next day, with a shrill ring that sliced through whatever calm I had willed into place. The man on the other end spoke impeccable English.

I must be in serious trouble if they've brought in someone who speaks better English than I do, I thought, and I began to measure the distance between my phone and the American Embassy.

No, he told me, he was not the censor. He was a representative from China's Committee for Educational Reform, a branch of the Ministry of Education.

"We have been following your progress," said the man.

"Well, yes, thank you," I said, remaining on guard.

"Would you consider creating a deportment curriculum for children in China's public school system?"

I asked the man to repeat himself. Not because I didn't hear him the first time, but because I could not fathom what he had just said. He confirmed the unfathomable: that the Chinese government—or some part of it—was asking me to teach Western manners to Chinese children.

My reaction swerved from confusion to astonishment and landed in a guttter of indecision.

I sought out colleagues for their advice. The government's request was surreal enough to inspire disbelief even among those who knew me well. True, I was a successful businesswoman, but I was hardly a spokeswoman for convention. My life featured a wide range of unorthodoxies that might well have helped me defy the laws of plausibility. How would I justify to the Chinese that which I find difficult to explain to Western colleagues? And did I really want to spend more time in China where there would continue to be unanswerable questions about its future?

More times than is probably sensible, I have been lured away from where I was by the unexplored of somewhere else. During the time I was writing my book in China, I discovered that China, the most paradoxical of nations, is not an easy place. In fact, with its remoteness and its newness, in its vagueness and its explicitness, China can be called unreasonable.

I am a reasonable person. It is in my nature. And because I came by it early, I've had years to observe that reason is often a repository of predictability with very little adventure to be found within its boundaries.

Nothing about agreeing to write a Western comportment program for Chinese children was remotely reasonable.

It was incongruous.

It was comical.

It was the last thing I expected.

And for all of those far more intriguing reasons than reason itself, I agreed to it.

EPILOGUE

Wherein I suggest it is always nice to know how to say good-bye

→ *FINAL LESSON*

Most conversations reach an obvious end when both people speaking to each other are ready to move on. If that is the case, the polite thing to say is "I've certainly enjoyed talking to you." If, however, you have been speaking to someone for a great while and wish to find an exit from the conversational cul-de-sac, smile at the person, extend your hand, and—even if neither is true—say, "Thank you for such an interesting conversation, but I think I should mingle with the other guests before I leave."

FURTHER READING

ON CHINA

Bonavia, David. *The Chinese.* London: Allen Lane / Penguin Books, 1981.

Doolittle, Justus. *Social Life of the Chinese.* London: Sampson Low, Son & Marston, 1866.

Du, Yongtao, and Jeff Kyong-McCain. *Chinese History in Geographical Perspective.* London: Lexington Books, 2013.

Fenby, Jonathan. *The Penguin History of Modern China: The Fall and Rise of a Great Power, 1850–2008.* London: Allen Lane / Penguin Books, 2008.

Ji, Zhaojin. *A History of Modern Shanghai Banking: The Rise and Decline of China's Financial Capital.* Armonk, N.Y.: M. E. Sharpe, 2003.

Werner, E. T. C. *China of the Chinese.* London: Sir Isaac Pitman & Sons, 1919.

ON ETIQUETTE

Post, Peggy, and Peter Post. *Emily Post's The Etiquette Advantage in Business: Personal Skills for Professional Success.* New York: Harper-Collins, 2005.

Tuckerman, Nancy, and Nancy Dunnan. *The Amy Vanderbilt Complete Book of Etiquette.* New York: Doubleday, 1995.

ACKNOWLEDGMENTS

I am indebted to Rebecca Carter, Lynn Nesbit, and Nan A. Talese.

My dutiful thanks for the coverage of China during my year living there by *The Economist,* the *Financial Times,* and *The New York Times.* Less factual but nonetheless insightful was *China Daily.*

My gratitude goes as well to the Athenaeum Club library in London and to the Society Library in New York.

My thanks are also due to friends and colleagues who have been generous with their expertise, time, and encouragement. In China, to Angela Chen, Jaime A. FlorCruz, Gilliam Collinsworth Hamilton, Jackie Huang, Heidi Park, Li Qin, and Sheri Yan; in London, to Matthew Evans, Susannah Fiennes, Victoria Greenwood, Mathias Hink, Michael Immordino, Tessa Keswick, Caryn Mandabach, Andrew Nurnberg, Deborah Owen, Kevin Pakenham, Ed Victor, and Xue Xinran; in New York, to Blythe Danner, Annabel Davis-Goff, John Fulvio, Cecilia Mendez Hodes, Gilbert C. Maurer, Kim McCarty, Michael McCarty, Frances Mitchell, Priscilla Morgan, and Pascal Volle.

A NOTE ABOUT THE AUTHOR

Eden Collinsworth is a former media executive and business consultant. She was the president and publisher of Arbor House Book Publishing Company in the 1980s. In 1990, she launched the Los Angeles–based monthly lifestyle magazine *Buzz,* after which she became vice president and director of cross-media business development at the Hearst Corporation. In 2008, she became vice president and chief of staff of an international think tank. In 2011, she launched Collinsworth & Associates, a consulting company, which specializes in intercultural communication. Her Chinese-language book *The Tao of Improving Your Likability: A Personal Guide to Effective Business Etiquette in Today's Global World* became a bestseller in mainland China.

A NOTE ABOUT THE TYPE

This book was set in Adobe Garamond. Designed for the Adobe Corporation by Robert Slimbach, the fonts are based on types first cut by Claude Garamond (c. 1480–1561). Garamond was a pupil of Geoffroy Tory's and is believed to have followed the Venetian models, although he introduced a number of important differences, and it is to him that we owe the letter we now know as "old style." He gave to his letters a certain elegance and feeling of movement that won their creator an immediate reputation and the patronage of Francis I of France.